10/03

27.45

WORLD
HISTORY SERIES ■ ■ ■

The History of Medicine

Titles in the World History Series

WORLD
HISTORY SERIES

The History of Medicine

by
Lisa Yount

Lucent Books, P.O. Box 289011, San Diego, CA 92198-9011

On cover: *The Doctor's Waiting Room*
by Vladimir Makovsky.

To Kat
for almost 40 years of fun and friendship.

Library of Congress Cataloging-in-Publication Data

Yount, Lisa.
    The history of medicine / by Lisa Yount.
       p. ; cm.—(World history series)
    Includes bibliographical references and index.
    Summary: Discusses the dawn of medicine, its
development into a science and ultimately into specialization,
and the challenges facing the current medical community.
    ISBN 1-56006-805-1 (lib. : alk. paper)
    1. Medicine—History—Juvenile literature. [1. Medicine—
History.]
    [DNLM: 1. History of Medicine—Juvenile Literature.
WZ 40 Y81h 2001] I. Title. II. Series.
    R133.5 .Y68 2002
    610'.9—dc21   2001000881

Contents

Foreword

Each year on the first day of school, nearly every history teacher faces the task of explaining why his or her students should study history. One logical answer to this question is that exploring what happened in our past explains how the things we often take for granted—our customs, ideas, and institutions—came to be. As statesman and historian Winston Churchill put it, "Every nation or group of nations has its own tale to tell. Knowledge of the trials and struggles is necessary to all who would comprehend the problems, perils, challenges, and opportunities which confront us today." Thus, a study of history puts modern ideas and institutions in perspective. For example, though the founders of the United States were talented and creative thinkers, they clearly did not invent the concept of democracy. Instead, they adapted some democratic ideas that had originated in ancient Greece and with which the Romans, the British, and others had experimented. An exploration of these cultures, then, reveals their very real connection to us through institutions that continue to shape our daily lives.

Another reason often given for studying history is the idea that lessons exist in the past from which contemporary societies can benefit and learn. This idea, although controversial, has always been an intriguing one for historians. Those who agree that society can benefit from the past often quote philosopher George Santayana's famous statement, "Those who cannot remember the past are condemned to repeat it." Historians who subscribe to Santayana's philosophy believe that, for example, studying the events that led up to the major world wars or other significant historical events would allow society to chart a different and more favorable course in the future.

Just as difficult as convincing students to realize the importance of studying history is the search for useful and interesting supplementary materials that present historical events in a context that can be easily understood. The volumes in Lucent Books' World History Series attempt to present a broad, balanced, and penetrating view of the march of history. Ancient Egypt's important wars and rulers, for example, are presented against the rich and colorful backdrop of Egyptian religious, social, and cultural developments. The series engages the reader by enhancing historical events with these cultural contexts. For example, in *Ancient Greece*, the text covers the role of women in that society. Slavery is discussed in *The Roman Empire*, as well as how slaves earned their freedom. The numerous and varied aspects of everyday life in these and other societies are explored in each volume of the series. Additionally, the series covers the major political, cultural, and philosophical ideas as the torch of civilization is passed from ancient Mesopotamia and Egypt, through Greece, Rome, Medieval Europe, and other world cultures, to the modern day.

The material in the series is formatted in a thorough, precise, and organized manner. Each volume offers the reader a comprehensive and clearly written overview of an important historical event or period. The topic under discussion is placed in a broad, historical context. For example, The Italian Renaissance begins with a discussion of the High Middle Ages and the loss of central control that allowed certain Italian cities to develop artistically. The book ends by looking forward to the Reformation and interpreting the societal changes that grew out of the Renaissance. Thus, students are not only involved in an historical era, but also enveloped by the events leading up to that era and the events following it.

One important and unique feature in the World History Series is the primary and secondary source quotations that richly supplement each volume. These quotes are useful in a number of ways. First, they allow students access to sources they would not normally be exposed to because of the difficulty and obscurity of the original source. The quotations range from interesting anecdotes to farsighted cultural perspectives and are drawn from historical witnesses both past and present. Second, the quotes demonstrate how and where historians themselves derive their information on the past as they strive to reach a consensus on historical events. Lastly, all of the quotes are footnoted, familiarizing students with the citation process and allowing them to verify quotes and/or look up the original source if the quote piques their interest.

Finally, the books in the World History Series provide a detailed launching point for further research. Each book contains a bibliography specifically geared toward student research. A second, annotated bibliography introduces students to all the sources the author consulted when compiling the book. A chronology of important dates gives students an overview, at a glance, of the topic covered. Where applicable, a glossary of terms is included.

In short, the series is designed not only to acquaint readers with the basics of history, but also to make them aware that their lives are a part of an ongoing human saga. Perhaps they will then come to the same realization as famed historian Arnold Toynbee. In his monumental work, *A Study of History*, he wrote about becoming aware of history flowing through him in a mighty current, and of his own life "welling like a wave in the flow of this vast tide."

IMPORTANT DATES IN THE HISTORY OF MEDICINE

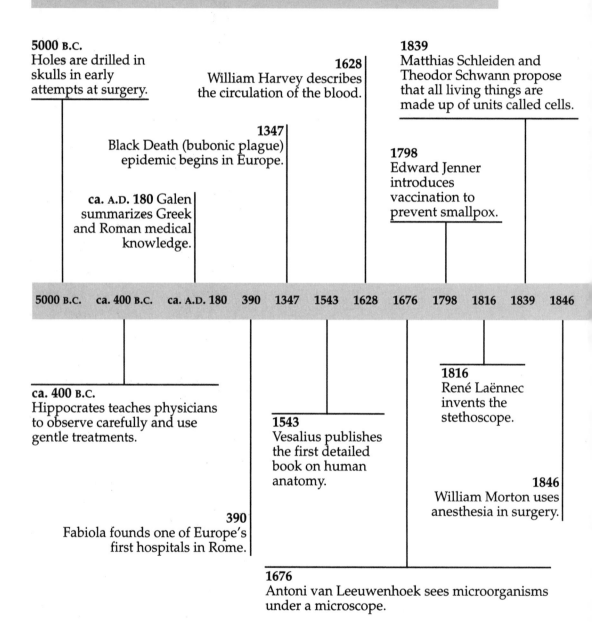

5000 B.C.
Holes are drilled in skulls in early attempts at surgery.

1628
William Harvey describes the circulation of the blood.

1839
Matthias Schleiden and Theodor Schwann propose that all living things are made up of units called cells.

1347
Black Death (bubonic plague) epidemic begins in Europe.

1798
Edward Jenner introduces vaccination to prevent smallpox.

ca. A.D. 180 Galen summarizes Greek and Roman medical knowledge.

| 5000 B.C. | ca. 400 B.C. | ca. A.D. 180 | 390 | 1347 | 1543 | 1628 | 1676 | 1798 | 1816 | 1839 | 1846 |

ca. 400 B.C.
Hippocrates teaches physicians to observe carefully and use gentle treatments.

1816
René Laënnec invents the stethoscope.

1543
Vesalius publishes the first detailed book on human anatomy.

1846
William Morton uses anesthesia in surgery.

390
Fabiola founds one of Europe's first hospitals in Rome.

1676
Antoni van Leeuwenhoek sees microorganisms under a microscope.

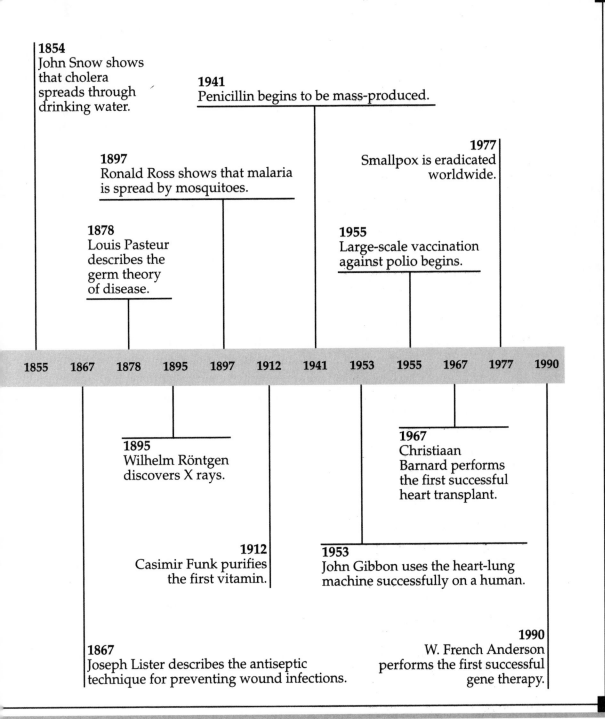

1854
John Snow shows that cholera spreads through drinking water.

1941
Penicillin begins to be mass-produced.

1897
Ronald Ross shows that malaria is spread by mosquitoes.

1977
Smallpox is eradicated worldwide.

1878
Louis Pasteur describes the germ theory of disease.

1955
Large-scale vaccination against polio begins.

| 1855 | 1867 | 1878 | 1895 | 1897 | 1912 | 1941 | 1953 | 1955 | 1967 | 1977 | 1990 |

1895
Wilhelm Röntgen discovers X rays.

1967
Christiaan Barnard performs the first successful heart transplant.

1912
Casimir Funk purifies the first vitamin.

1953
John Gibbon uses the heart-lung machine successfully on a human.

1867
Joseph Lister describes the antiseptic technique for preventing wound infections.

1990
W. French Anderson performs the first successful gene therapy.

Healing, Medicine, and Science

Since the dawn of human existence, there have been healers: people who, in addition to their everyday occupations, tried to cure the sick and injured, or at least care for them and make them feel better. About 4,000 years ago, after people had come to live in communities and divide their labor, some healers began to define themselves as a separate profession. These individuals became known as physicians, and their profession was called medicine. As scientific research developed in Europe in the fifteenth and sixteenth centuries, the discoveries of scientists in laboratories added to the knowledge and techniques that physicians could use in treating sick people.

Healing, medicine, and science overlap, but for centuries they did not communicate with each other very well. When the profession of medicine gained prestige in the late Middle Ages, university-trained physicians started to turn away from other healers. They insisted that surgeons and apothecaries (druggists), for example, be accorded less prestige than themselves. They barred women and some other groups from medicine entirely. In doing so, physicians both held these other healers back and cut themselves off from practical knowledge offered by these individuals.

RESISTANCE TO SCIENCE

Most physicians were also slow to learn from science. Doctors often went on believing outmoded theories that they had learned in medical school long after scientists had proved these ideas wrong. For example, scientists in the sixteenth, seventeenth, and eighteenth centuries learned a great deal about the structure of the human body and the way it worked, but their discoveries had little effect on everyday medicine until dozens, sometimes hundreds, of years after they were made.

All this finally began to change in the nineteenth century. Surgeons and pharmacists (professionals who make and sell drugs or medications) worked more closely with physicians than before and gained in prestige. In the second half of the century, women won the right to train as physicians. Perhaps most important, medicine forged a powerful alliance with science. Physicians worked in laboratories themselves or followed closely the studies of others who did. As a result, medical progress, which in pre-

A fifteenth-century Italian fresco shows apothecaries at work in a pharmacy well stocked with drugs. Pharmacists of this time were not as respected as physicians.

vious centuries had been slow, suddenly began to make great strides. Physicians learned the true cause of many diseases and how to prevent them. Surgeons became able to operate without causing their patients pain and with much less risk of starting life-threatening infections.

Progress accelerated in the twentieth century. Physicians and scientific researchers worked together to develop ways to cure many infectious diseases (those caused by microorganisms such as bacteria and viruses). They made progress in understanding, preventing, and treating other illnesses, such as cancer and heart disease. They worked with government and private groups to prevent sickness by improving the conditions under which most people in

In 1849 Elizabeth Blackwell became the first woman to receive a medical degree in the United States. Up until the mid-1800s, women were barred from practicing medicine.

developed countries lived. Largely because of these efforts, people in the United States could, by the end of the century, expect to live an average of 76.1 years, compared to a life expectancy a hundred years earlier of only 47.3 years.

Practicing physicians and laboratory scientists are likely to cooperate more closely than ever during the twenty-first century. Researchers hope to find more effective ways to treat or even cure heart disease, cancer, Alzheimer's disease, and other major destroyers of human life and health. Physicians may become able to prevent or control some illnesses by changing genes, the very blueprint of life. Increasingly, too, physicians are learning from other healers, including those who use knowledge that has not been part of traditional Western medicine. When healers, physicians, and scientists all work together—or, as increasingly happens, these three professions are combined in the same individuals—medicine's power to help humanity may know few limits.

Chapter

1 The Dawn of Medicine

Sickness, injury, and death have always been part of life—but not a part that humans like to accept. From earliest times, some people no doubt tried to head off or reverse these tragedies. Therefore, medicine —attempts to identify, treat, and prevent disease—is probably as old as humanity.

THE EARLIEST HEALERS

No one knows who the first healers were or exactly what they did. Archaeologists suspect, however, that they combined treatment of the body with religion. Illness and injury often strike without warning, so early humans, like people in many later cultures, most likely believed that such disasters were caused by evil spirits or angry gods. Religious specialists called shamans took on the task of dealing with these supernatural beings. (A seventeen-thousand-year-old cave painting in France shows a man in a deer mask who archaeologists think is a shaman.)

Besides calling on shamans' prayers and magic spells, early humans most likely took down-to-earth steps to protect their health. Biologists have seen monkeys and apes seek out and eat certain plants that are not part of their normal diet. Substances in these plants kill tiny parasites that can make the animals sick. Early humans probably made similar discoveries. Men also no doubt tried to slow bleeding from wounds by pressing or wrapping them. Women helped one another give birth.

In skeletons dating from the New Stone Age, some seven thousand years ago, archaeologists have found signs of attempts to promote healing. Broken bones have healed straight, suggesting that splints of some kind were used to support them. Skulls have holes that were drilled in them in what may have been the world's first surgery. Some skulls contain several such holes, surrounded by bone that grew after the holes were made. This proves not only that the operations were carried out on living people but that, amazingly, the patients survived and even let the process be repeated.

MEDICINE BECOMES A PROFESSION

The first recorded information about medicine comes from an area in modern-day

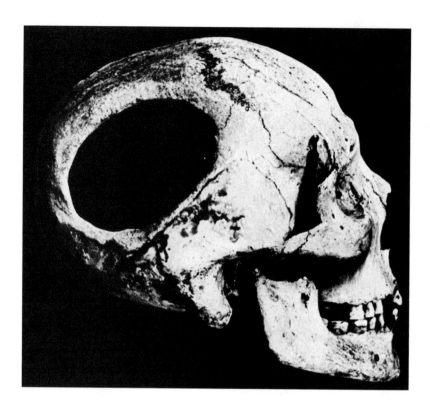

Humans in the New Stone Age performed some of the world's first surgeries by drilling holes in living patients' skulls, possibly to relieve pressure on the brain.

Iraq between the Tigris and Euphrates Rivers. Archaeologists call this spot Mesopotamia, meaning "land between the rivers." A series of civilizations grew up here starting more than five thousand years ago, and several left writings that refer to illness and its treatment. The oldest of these may be a clay tablet dating from around 2150 B.C. that describes the washing and bandaging of wounds. Tablets from a civilization called Assyria, written in the seventh century B.C., describe many diseases and their likely outcomes. They also list medical uses for hundreds of plant, animal, and mineral substances.

Many healers in Mesopotamia were also priests. However, physicians—those who practice medicine and who use natural rather than supernatural treatments—were starting to be seen as a separate profession. Hammurabi, a king of a late Mesopotamian civilization called Babylonia, left a law code carved on a huge stone pillar, and 10 of its 282 laws relate to medicine. Some list payments that physicians were to receive for doing surgery on patients of different classes. Other laws describe the penalties that the physicians would suffer if the patients died.

The civilization of ancient Egypt overlapped the Mesopotamian ones and grew even more powerful. Archaeologists have found scrolls of papyrus, a paperlike material made from reeds, containing several Egyptian writings on medicine. One, the Georg Ebers papyrus, dates from around 1550 B.C. but probably copies information that is much older. It describes dozens of diseases and their treatments, including both magic spells and some seven hundred drugs ranging from pomegranates to hippopotamus fat. The Edwin Smith papyrus, written about 1600 B.C., covers surgery, which mostly consisted of treating injuries such as wounds and broken bones.

An engraved black basalt stele bears the Code of Hammurabi, a collection of 282 laws dating from the first half of the eighteenth century B.C.

The most famous Egyptian physician of whom records remain is Imhotep, who lived around 2600 B.C. This man of many talents was also the vizier (prime minister) of his pharaoh, Zoser, and designed the king's burial pyramid. Imhotep gained such renown that in later times he was worshiped as a god. The names of several hundred other Egyptian physicians have been preserved as well. The ancient Greek historian Herodotus wrote that by his time, the fifth century B.C., "all places [in Egypt] abound[ed] in physicians."[1] Some were even specialists, treating only certain diseases or problems in a single part of the body such as the eyes.

INDIAN AND CHINESE MEDICINE

While medicine was beginning in Mesopotamia and Egypt, medical traditions also developed in India and China. Many of these are still followed. The best-known system of traditional Indian medicine is called Ayurveda, which means "the knowledge needed for long life." It includes beliefs based on both of India's oldest chief religions, Hinduism and Buddhism. The first surviving writings on Ayurvedic medicine date from the early centuries A.D., but they may contain knowledge that is much older.

The chief Ayurvedic works are medical encyclopedias supposed to have been written by two sages, or wise men. One sage, Charaka, is said to have lived around 100 A.D. Susruta, the other, came about two hundred years later. Charaka's and Susruta's works tell physicians how to diagnose disease, or find out its cause and nature, by studying the patient's appearance, listening to sounds in the chest and abdomen, and gently pressing or squeezing the body. The works list 341 plant medicines, 177 medicines made from animals, and 64 from minerals. They also describe surgical treatments, including a type of plastic surgery that reshapes a flap of skin from a person's forehead to replace a missing nose. This was a useful operation because cutting off the nose was a punishment for several types of crime.

The roots of Chinese medicine, like those of other ancient medical traditions, are buried in myth. China's earliest med-ical books are supposed to have been written by three legendary emperors. The most extensive, the *Inner Canon of Medicine*, is credited to Yu Hsing, the Yellow Emperor, who is said to have lived around 2600 B.C. The *Inner Canon* was first written down soon after China became politically unified in 221 B.C.

Chinese and Indian medicine share a belief that is also found in many other cultures. They say that health results from being in harmony with oneself and one's surroundings. The harmony within a healthy body is thought to mirror the balance that is supposed to exist in nature

A seventh-century B.C. figurine of the ancient Egyptian physician Imhotep.

PAYMENTS AND PENALTIES

Around 1700 B.C., Hammurabi, a powerful king of Babylonia (an area now part of Iraq), had his kingdom's law code carved on a giant stone pillar. In Medicine: An Illustrated History, *Albert S. Lyons and R. Joseph Petrucelli reprint some of the ten laws that affected physicians.*

"If a doctor has treated a freeman [upper-class citizen] with a metal knife for a severe wound, and has cured the freeman, or has opened a freeman's tumor with a metal knife, and cured a freeman's eye, then he shall receive ten shekels of silver.

If [the patient is] the son of a plebeian [lower-class citizen], he [the doctor] shall receive five shekels of silver.

If [the patient is] a man's slave, the owner of the slave shall give two shekels of silver to the doctor.

If a doctor has treated a man with a metal knife for a severe wound, and has caused the man to die, or has opened a man's tumor with a metal knife and destroyed the man's eye, his hands shall be cut off.

If a doctor has treated the slave of a plebeian with a metal knife for a severe wound and has caused him to die, he shall render [give] slave for slave.

If he has opened his tumor with a metal knife and destroyed his eye, he shall pay half his price in silver."

---

or a well-run nation. The *Inner Canon* states, for example,

A human body is the counterpart of a state [nation]. . . . The spirit [the body's governing vitalities] is like the monarch; the blood . . . is like the ministers; the *qi* [energy] is like the people. Thus we know that one who keeps his own body in order can keep a state in order. Loving care for one's people is what makes it possible for a state to be secure; nurturing one's *qi* is what makes it possible to keep the body intact.[2]

According to this belief, illness occurs when the body's inner harmony is disturbed. This may happen by chance or may be caused by a person's own unwise actions or factors in the environment. The physician's job is to restore harmony by means of religious ritual, physical treatments, or both. Better still, the physician should teach people how to maintain harmony in the first place. "The superior physician helps before the early budding of disease,"[3] the Yellow Emperor is supposed to have written.

The basic idea underlying Chinese medicine is that a form of energy or spirit called *qi* or *chi* flows through the body along certain paths. Sickness results when the flow of the body's *qi* is disturbed or blocked, or when harmful *qi* enters from outside. The disturbance in the flow of *qi* is caused by an imbalance between two qualities, yin and yang. Yin is said to be feminine, dark, passive, moist, and cold. Yang is yin's exact opposite: masculine, light, active, dry, and hot.

Chinese medical treatments aim to remove harmful *qi* and stop its effects. They also build up healthy *qi* and restore its proper flow by repairing the imbalance between yin and yang. The treatment best known today is probably acupuncture, which was first described in a text supposed to have been written around 2800 B.C. In acupuncture, needles are put into the body at certain spots to redirect the body's *qi*. The needles are then twirled and vibrated. Acupuncture has become popular in the West as well as in Asia.

Chinese physicians identified diseases through techniques such as studying the patient's pulse, or heartbeat, which can be felt at the wrist and other spots on the body. One ancient text stated, "The human body is likened to a chord instrument, of which the different pulses are the chords. The harmony or discord of the organism can be recognized by examining the pulse, which is thus fundamental for all medicine."[4] However, it was not thought proper for physicians, who were always men, to examine the bodies of women patients. Therefore, women used small porcelain dolls to explain their problems. They pointed to the parts of the doll that matched the parts of their bodies that hurt.

HIPPOCRATES

The ancient beliefs that had the greatest effect on Western medicine came from Greece. At first, like other early cultures, the Greeks blamed the gods for illness and looked to them for healing. One of these healer gods, Asklepios, was sometimes combined or confused with Egypt's Imhotep. Asklepios was often pictured carrying a staff with a snake twined around it, a symbol still often used in Western cultures to represent medicine. Sick people came to the god's temples, which were widespread by the fourth century B.C., and slept there

Acupuncture has been practiced in China for over four thousand years and is becoming increasingly common in the West as well.

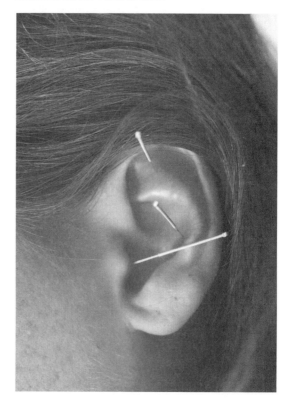

THE IMPORTANCE OF WESTERN MEDICINE

In The Greatest Benefit to Mankind: A Medical History of Humanity, *Roy Porter explains why his book, like most histories of medicine, focuses chiefly on Western medicine (the medicine of Europe and North America).*

"Western medicine has developed in ways which have made it uniquely powerful and led it to become uniquely global. . . . There is every reason to expect the medicine of the future to be an outgrowth of present western medicine—or at least a reaction against it. What began as the medicine of Europe is becoming the medicine of humanity. For that reason its history deserves particular attention. . . .

Whereas most traditional healing systems have sought to understand the relations of the sick person to the wider cosmos [universe] and to make readjustments between individual and world, or society and world, the western medical tradition explains sickness principally in terms of the body itself—its own cosmos. [Ancient] Greek medicine dismissed supernatural powers, though not . . . environmental influences; and from the Renaissance the flourishing anatomical and physiological programmes [research on the structure and functions of the body] created a new confidence among investigators that everything that needed to be known could essentially be discovered by probing more deeply and ever more minutely into the flesh, its systems, tissues, cells, its DNA.

This has proved to be an infinitely productive inquiry, generating first knowledge and then power, including on some occasions the power to conquer disease. The idea of probing into bodies, living and dead (and especially *human* bodies) with a view to improving medicine is more or less distinctive to the European medical tradition."

overnight. The god was expected to visit them in a dream, or what seemed like a dream, and prescribe or carry out treatment. Temple priests probably acted the part of Asklepios.

Some Greek thinkers, however, developed the belief that nature was strictly physical and did not need supernatural explanations. All causes of illness, they said, lay in the body and its earthly environment. These thinkers can be said to be the first scientists.

Hippocrates, the most famous Greek physician, shared this belief. Historians

Hippocrates believed that doctors should observe patients' symptoms and lifestyles to truly understand their medical conditions.

think Hippocrates lived from about 460 to 377 B.C. Little is known about his life except that he seems to have taught and practiced medicine on the island of Cos. About sixty writings credited to him have been preserved, but no one knows which ones, if any, he really composed. They include books on the philosophy of medicine, textbooks, and notes about particular patients.

Hippocrates and his followers believed that the human body and its illnesses could be understood by observing and reasoning. Studying the patient and his or her environment was especially important:

> A great part . . . of the Art [of medicine] is to be able to observe. . . . Ob-
> serve the nature of each country; diet; customs; the age of the patient; speech; manners; fashion; even his silence; his thoughts; if he sleeps or is suffering from lack of sleep; the content and origin of his dreams. . . . One has to study all these signs and to analyze what they portend [mean].[5]

AN IMBALANCE OF HUMORS

Like most Greeks, Hippocrates and his students thought that all nature was made up of four elements: fire, water, air, and earth. The human body was supposed to contain four liquids, or humors, that corresponded to these elements: blood, phlegm, yellow bile, and black bile. Each humor had several qualities. Blood, for example, was warm and moist. Black bile was cold and dry.

Hippocratic physicians, like Indian and Chinese ones, believed that health was a matter of harmony or balance. A healthy person's body contained exactly the right amount of each of the four humors. Too much of a humor in a certain part of the body threw off the balance and made the person sick. This imbalance could be caused by factors such as personal habits, diet, activity, climate, or surroundings. Western physicians would go on believing this ancient Greek theory for more than two thousand years.

Hippocrates and his followers tried to correct imbalances in the body by removing excess humors. They might take blood from a patient, for instance, or make the person vomit. Such actions were to be taken, however, only if they seemed safe:

The first principle of Hippocratic medicine was "do no harm."[6] Mild treatments such as changes in diet were the most preferred, followed by other remedies in order of harshness. One Hippocratic writing stated, "What drugs fail to cure, that the knife [surgery] cures; what the knife cures not, that the fire [burning to stop bleeding or remove tumors] cures; but what fire fails to cure, this must be called incurable."[7] Hippocratic physicians felt that most healing should be left to nature.

Better than trying to repair an imbalance of humors, Hippocratic physicians said, was keeping the imbalance from occurring in the first place. This could be done by persuading people to follow a healthy lifestyle. Hippocratic advice for maintaining health is much like the advice many doctors give today: Eat moderately, exercise regularly, keep clean, and reduce stress. Medical writings from India and China list similar recommendations.

THE SCIENTIFIC METHOD

Another ancient Greek thinker who affected later medicine was Aristotle, who lived from about 384 to 322 B.C. He created what has come to be called the scientific method. In this approach to learning, people observe some part of nature and suggest an explanation for what they see. They then test the explanation by observing further or carrying out experiments. Finally, if needed, they change the explanation to fit the new facts they have learned and then test it again. This method lies at the root of all Western science.

One kind of experiment that Aristotle performed was dissection, or cutting open dead animals. He was the first to use dissection regularly as a tool for learning about the structure and functions of the body. He did not dissect humans because the Greeks, like the Indians, the Chinese, and many other cultures, believed that doing so was wrong. Instead, he dissected animals and used what he learned about their bodies to make guesses about human anatomy, or body structure. Many of his guesses were wrong, because human bodies are not exactly like those of animals. The technique he pioneered, however, would prove very useful in future centuries.

Fourth-century B.C. Greek philosopher Aristotle developed the scientific method, the basis of all Western science.

GREEK MEDICINE COMES TO ROME

When control of the Mediterranean world passed from Greece to Rome around 146 B.C., Greek physicians imported their medical ideas into Roman civilization. Some Romans disapproved of these ideas or disliked the Greek doctors, who often were or had been slaves. Over time, however, experts such as Asklepiades, who promised to cure illness "swiftly, safely, sweetly"[8] with gentle Hippocratic treatments, won the Romans over. Roman writers such as Celsus, who lived around the time of Christ and wrote an eight-volume medical

---

AN HONORABLE PHYSICIAN

The most famous writing credited to the ancient Greek physician Hippocrates is the Hippocratic oath, a statement of medical ethics that many doctors still recite when graduating from medical school. This excerpt from the oath, translated by J. Chadwick and N. Mann, appears in The Cambridge Illustrated History of Medicine, *edited by Roy Porter.*

"I swear by Apollo the healer, by Aesculapius, by Health and all the powers of healing, and call to witness all the gods and goddesses that I may keep this Oath and Promise to the best of my ability and judgement. . . .

I will use my power to help the sick to the best of my ability and judgement; I will abstain from harming or wronging any man by it.

I will not give a fatal drought [drug] to anyone if I am asked, nor will I suggest any such thing. Neither will I give a woman means to procure an abortion.

I will be chaste and religious in my life and in my practice.

I will not cut [perform surgery], even for the stone [bladder stones], but I will leave such procedures to the practitioners of that craft.

Whenever I go into a house, I will go to help the sick and never with the intention of doing harm or injury. I will not abuse my position. . . .

Whatever I see or hear, professionally or privately, which ought not to be divulged [revealed], I will keep secret and tell no one.

If, therefore, I observe this Oath and do not violate it, may I prosper both in my life and in my profession, earning good repute [respect] among all men for all time. If I transgress and forswear [break] this Oath, may my lot [fortune] be otherwise."

---

encyclopedia, preserved and added to the Greeks' ideas. A few decades later another Roman, Dioscorides, wrote the first detailed book on medicinal plants.

GALEN

The best-known Roman physician and medical writer was Galen, who lived from about A.D. 129 to 216. Galen was born in Pergamum (now Bergama, Turkey), part of the Greek world that Rome controlled. His wealthy father gave him a fine education and steered him toward medicine after dreaming that Asklepios asked him to do so.

Galen is said to have written three books before he was thirteen years old. He went on to study in Alexandria, Egypt, then the Mediterranean's chief center of learning. When he came back to Pergamum, he became a physician to the city's gladiators, trained fighters who battled each other to amuse the citizens. The many injuries Galen treated during this job added to his knowledge of surgery and human anatomy. In 162, he went to Rome and soon became well known there. He even treated the emperor, Marcus Aurelius. Galen wrote dozens, perhaps even hundreds, of books describing Greek ideas about medicine and adding his own.

Galen stressed that physicians should learn their trade by observing for themselves, not just by reading books. Like Aristotle, he dissected animals such as apes, goats, sheep, and pigs and tried to apply the results to the human body. He adopted the Greek belief in the four humors, but he had more faith in drugs than the Greeks

The writings of ancient Roman physician Galen shaped the course of European medicine for fifteen centuries.

did. One of his favorites was a mixture called theriac, which had been used long before his time as a treatment for snakebite. Theriac came to be used to counteract any kind of poison or, indeed, almost any disease. Galen's version of it had more than seventy ingredients. This complex remedy was useless, but amazingly, forms of it would remain on druggists' books until the late nineteenth century.

Galen had a great range of knowledge, a high opinion of the medical profession, and an even higher opinion of himself. "It is I, and I alone, who have revealed the true path of medicine," he wrote. "It must be admitted that Hippocrates already staked

STUDYING THE BODY

The ancient Roman physician Galen, whose works remained the chief medical authority in Europe for more than a thousand years, told physicians to learn about the structure of the body by cutting up, or dissecting, the dead bodies of humans and animals. His advice, taken from an essay on bones, appears in the Source Book of Medical History, *edited by Logan Clendening, who also translated this essay.*

"The human bones are subjects of study with which you should . . . become perfectly familiar. You cannot merely read about the bones in . . . books . . . such as this my own book; which is much more reliable and exact than any previously written on the subject. Pursue by hard study, then, not only the descriptions of the bones in the book, but also acquaint yourself with the appearance of each of the bones, by the use of your own eyes handling each bone by itself so that you become a first-hand observer.

At Alexandria [Egypt] this is very easy, since the physicians in that country accompany the instruction they give to their students with opportunities for personal inspection (at autopsy [dissection of bodies after death]). Hence you must try to get to Alexandria. . . . But if you cannot manage this, still it is not impossible to obtain a view of human bones. Personally I have very often had a chance to do this where tombs or monuments have become broken up. . . .

Even if you do not have the luck to see anything like this, still you can dissect an ape, and learn each of the bones from it, by carefully removing the flesh. For this purpose you must choose apes which most resemble man. Such are those in whom the jaws are not prominent nor the canine teeth large. In such apes you will also find the other parts as in man, whence they walk and run on two legs."

out this path. . . . He prepared the way, but I have made it passable."[9] An excellent as well as prolific writer, Galen seemingly had no trouble persuading others to share his belief that he knew the answers to all possible medical questions. He would remain the chief European authority on medicine for the next fifteen hundred years.

2 Rebirth

Galen's confidence in his profession no doubt seemed comforting to people in the troubled centuries during which the Roman Empire's strength slowly faded. The Visigoths, a Germanic people, invaded Rome in A.D. 410. By then, what was left of Rome's power had shifted to what became known as the Byzantine Empire, centered in Constantinople (now Istanbul, Turkey). In Western Europe, the remains of the old empire slowly collapsed into isolated settlements.

A Time of Religion

After about the seventh century, scholarship, medical and otherwise, almost ceased in most of Europe. The idea of trusting one's own senses and reasoning fell out of favor in those uncertain times. Instead, most people turned to religion for guidance in their lives. Christianity, merely an often-persecuted sect in Galen's day, had slowly gained popularity and had become the state religion of the Byzantine Empire in the early fifth century. During the Middle Ages—the time from about the fifth to the fifteenth century—the Christian Church held the real

power in Europe, both in politics and in people's daily existence.

Early Christianity, like the Jewish faith from which it descended, held that illness was usually God's punishment for sin. At the same time, it saw helping sick people as a merciful and noble act. The Bible showed Jesus as a supernatural healer. It also told stories such as that of the Good Samaritan, who selflessly helped an injured stranger.

Taking these stories to heart, some Christians set up institutions to house the sick and poor. Around 390, for instance, a wealthy Roman woman named Fabiola converted to Christianity. She then established one of Europe's first hospitals in Rome. Her teacher, known today as St. Jerome, wrote,

> She assembled all the sick from the streets and highways and personally tended the unhappy and impoverished victims of hunger and disease. I have often seen her washing wounds which others—even men—could hardly bear to look at. . . . She founded a hospital and gathered there the sufferers from the streets, and gave them all the attentions of a nurse.[10]

Constantinople later boasted several large hospitals. One had more than two hundred beds, with separate wards for such specialties as surgery and treatment of eye diseases.

Some Christian religious groups made caring for sick people a major part of their work. For example, St. Benedict, who in 529 established what would become one of the most important orders of Roman Catholic monks, wrote that, for this group, "the care of the sick is to be placed above and before every other duty."[11] Indeed, most physicians between about the eighth and tenth centuries were monks or others closely tied to the church.

Some monasteries preserved and copied ancient medical texts such as the works of Galen. Not all medical monks read these books, however. Instead they often confined their efforts to simply keeping the sick comfortable. Benedict, for example, ordered his monks not to study medicine because he felt that sickness could be cured only by God. Partly as a result, much Greek and Roman medical knowledge was lost to Western Europe during the early Middle Ages.

St. Benedict, founder of the Benedictine order of monks. St. Benedict believed that care of the sick was vital for monks, yet he discouraged the formal study of medicine.

This drawing depicts Persian physician and alchemist Rhazes, who lived from 867 to 925, at work in his laboratory in Baghdad.

In the Middle East, however, practitioners of another religion, Islam, preserved medical knowledge. Believers in Islam, called Muslims, became powerful in the seventh century and spread their culture and religion to North Africa, Spain, and part of France.

PRESERVERS OF KNOWLEDGE

Muslims valued learning highly. Starting in the eighth century, Muslims—and Jewish and Christian scholars as well—living in cities such as Baghdad translated many ancient Greek and Roman works, including Galen's books, into Arabic. Muslim master physicians such as Abu-Bakr Muhammad ibn Zakariya ar-Razi (Rhazes) and Abu-Ali al-Husayn ibn Abdallah ibn Sina (Avicenna) added their own experience and philosophy to these translated books. The results were learned encyclopedias that became vital parts of every physician's library. Jewish physicians working in Muslim countries, such as Rabbi Moses ben Maimon (Maimonides), wrote their own encyclopedias in Hebrew and Arabic.

A miniature from the Canon Maior, *a book by Islamic physician Avicenna, depicts a scene in a pharmacy.*

European scholars learned of these works when they came to Muslim-controlled cities such as Cordoba in Spain. They in turn translated the encyclopedias into Latin, which most educated Europeans could read. Sometimes the books were also translated into more common European languages such as French or English.

Muslims gave more to medicine than just books. As al-Razi wrote at the time, "All that is written in books is worth much less than the experience of a wise doctor."[12] Like the Christians, the Muslims valued caring for the sick and needy. They set up large hospitals in Cairo (Egypt), Baghdad (now in Iraq), and elsewhere. Muslim physicians were experts on drugs, and the first pharmacies, businesses devoted to making and selling medicines, appeared in Muslim countries.

MEDICAL SCHOOLS

Life improved for many Europeans as the second millennium began. The continent's population grew during the twelfth and thirteenth centuries, and more people came to live in cities. A new middle class prospered by trading and, in turn, enriched others.

During these relatively comfortable times, interest in education revived, and medicine began to separate itself from religion once again. As part of this movement, the church forbade monks to practice medicine (at least for pay) in 1163. Many religious orders turned their hospitals over to city governments. At the same time, for the first time since ancient Greece and Rome, nonreligious schools for training physicians arose. One of the first and most famous was in the southern Italian town of Salerno. According to legend, Salerno's medical school had been founded by four scholars: one Latin, one Greek, one Arabic, and one Jewish. Whether or not these wise men really existed, the backgrounds claimed for them showed the wide range of cultures that shaped learning in the school.

Salerno was unusual in that it admitted women, and women as well as men taught medicine in Salerno. One woman teacher, Trotula, wrote a textbook on childbirth and women's diseases that was used throughout Europe for hundreds of years. In most parts of Europe, women were barred from medical schools. Indeed, they were sometimes forbidden from practicing medicine and could work only as nurses or midwives (women who helped other women give birth). These bans would remain in effect until the mid–nineteenth century.

By the middle of the twelfth century, other famous medical schools had grown up in such cities as Paris; Bologna, Italy; and Oxford, England. Students in these schools had to study for ten years before they could become physicians. Mostly they memorized the works of Galen and other authorities. They also dissected animals and, if they were lucky, saw one or two dissections of the bodies of executed criminals each year. Surgeons, who at that time were not held in high regard, did the actual cutting in these demonstrations. A professor, meanwhile, sat on a platform and read Galen's descriptions of what the students were supposed to see.

In recognition of their education, physicians who had graduated from medical schools began to be called "doctor." They were greatly respected, and their patients most often were nobles or rich merchants' families. Physicians looked down on other healers who had less training, such as midwives or surgeons, who often doubled as barbers. Around the twelfth century, to protect what they saw as the standards of their profession, physicians formed organizations called guilds to test graduating doctors and oversee medical practice. Some countries required physicians to be tested by medical school professors before they could treat patients.

THE BLACK DEATH

Some illnesses were beyond the capabilities of physicians, however. Not even the most learned doctors could halt the disastrous epidemic of bubonic plague called the Black Death. Soldiers and traders brought the disease from Asia in 1347, and in less than five years it killed about a fourth of Europe's population. One Italian who survived the plague wrote,

Father abandoned child, wife husband, one brother another. . . . None could be found to bury the dead for money or friendship. . . . They [plague victims] died by the hundreds, both day and night, and all were thrown in ditches and covered with earth. And as soon as those ditches were filled, more were dug. And I, Agnolo di Tura . . . buried my five children with my own hands.[13]

People at the time did not know it, but the plague was really a sickness of rats. Fleas transmitted the plague bacteria when they bit rats to feed on their blood.

SOUND HEALTH ADVICE

Doctors at the famous medical school in Salerno, Italy, wrote a long poem containing advice on how to stay healthy that remained popular for hundreds of years. This excerpt, taken from Sir John Harington's 1608 translation, appears in Logan Clendening's Source Book of Medical History.

"The Salerno School doth by these lines impart [wish]
All health to England's King, and doth advise
From care [worry] his head to keep, from wrath [anger]
   his heart,
Drink not much wine, sup light [eat little at dinner], and
   soon arise,
When meat is gone, long sitting breedeth smart [harm]:
And after noon still waking keep your eyes.
When moved you find yourself to Nature's needs
Forbear [avoid] them not, for that much danger breeds,
Use three Physicians still; first Doctor Quiet,
Next Doctor Merry-man, and Doctor Diet. . . .

Yet for your lodging rooms give this direction,
In houses where you mind to make your dwelling,
That near the same there be no evil scents
Of puddle-waters, or of excrements,
Let air be clear and light, and free from faults,
That come of secret passages and vaults. . . .

Against these several humors overflowing,
As several kinds of Physic [medicine] may be good,
As diet, drink, hot baths, whence sweat is growing,
With purging, vomiting, and letting [removing] blood:
Which taken in due time, not overflowing,
Each malady's [disease's] infection is withstood."

A woodcut from 1520 shows a doctor's visit to a plague victim. Europe was first hit by the plague in 1347 and suffered additional outbreaks in the following centuries.

If too many rats died, the fleas would infest and bite humans instead; in doing so, the tiny insects spread the disease to them. Infected people developed dark bruises on their skin and swellings, or buboes, under their arms and elsewhere on their bodies. They often died within days. Worse still, the disease sometimes took another form called pneumonic plague. This form, which affected the lungs, could be spread directly from person to person by coughing and sneezing.

Physicians could not decide whether the plague was spread by contact with sick people or by "bad air." Both of these theories about epidemic diseases—diseases that strike many people at once—went back to the Greeks and Romans. Doctors who thought the sickness was contagious, or spread by contact, advised leaving the crowded cities. Physicians as well as others acted on a popular saying: "Flee quickly, go far, come back slowly."[14]

As another alternative, local governments tried to keep potentially sick strangers out of uninfected towns. The Italian seaport of Venice, for instance, required arriving ships, crews, and goods to remain outside the city for forty days (*quaranti giorni*) to allow time for signs of plague to appear. The word *quarantine*, meaning the isolation of sick people to stop the spread of disease, came from this restriction. Venice's ruling was an early example of public health laws that governments used to try to prevent or control disease.

Doctors who believed in the "bad air" theory, on the other hand, thought that the plague was caused or spread by poisons given off by rotting matter. They advised cleaning houses and filling them with sweet-smelling or strong-smelling substances to keep the poisons out. Some of these physicians tried to protect themselves by wearing leather gowns and birdlike masks packed with herbs when they treated plague victims. Like physicians' other efforts to combat the plague, this seldom did much good.

REBIRTH

The Black Death and other epidemics, along with famines and wars, destroyed the optimism of Europe's people. For a while, they returned to the belief that religion was their only hope in a chaotic world. As the sixteenth century began, however, Europe felt a new burst of energy and creativity known today as the Renaissance. This rebirth of learning and culture was fueled by new inventions, especially the printing press, created by Johannes Gutenberg in what is now Germany around 1450. Thanks to this device, many identical copies of books could be made far more quickly and cheaply than before. New wealth brought to Europe from Asia and from the recently rediscovered Americas also encouraged this "rebirth."

The knowledge of ancient Greece and Rome was what Renaissance scholars wanted to see reborn. They studied the works of ancient authors, including medical books, in their original Greek, rather than in the translations made during the late Middle Ages. By doing so, they hoped to avoid the mistakes that had crept in as the works were translated and recopied by hand. One medical scholar of the time said that because of this new approach, "medicine had been raised from the dead."[15]

Renaissance thinkers also rediscovered ways of thinking that had been all but forgotten during the Middle Ages. Instead of taking the word of ancient experts such as Galen, they began to rely on their own observations—as Galen himself had advised. Instead of focusing on God, the afterlife, and the soul, they turned to the earthly world of humanity and nature.

A MEDICAL RULEBREAKER

One of the most colorful of the thinkers who tried to move beyond ancient authorities was a Swiss man named Theophrastus Bombastus von Hohenheim. He boastingly called himself Paracelsus, meaning "better than" Celsus, the famous Roman medical encyclopedist. Paracelsus liked to make statements such as "One hair on my neck knows more than all you authors, and my shoe-buckles contain more wisdom than both Galen and Avicenna."[16] (That might have amused Galen, who had an equally immodest view of himself. No wonder Paracelsus's middle name later entered English as *bombast*, a word meaning boastful talk.)

Paracelsus wandered all over Europe, the Middle East, and even Russia. In keeping with his opinion of scholars, he sought knowledge from the folk healers whom

Swiss physician Paracelsus broke with the prevailing medical views and consulted folk healers to expand his knowledge.

university-trained physicians scorned. "I have not been ashamed to learn from tramps, butchers, and barbers,"[17] he wrote. He also studied astrology, the forerunner of astronomy, and alchemy, the forerunner of chemistry. These subjects were full of mystical beliefs, and Paracelsus's own writings contain as much of magic as they do of science.

Still, Paracelsus made important contributions to medicine. He introduced many new drugs, especially ones made from metals and minerals such as mercury, copper, and arsenic. He was one of the first to apply chemistry to medicine. His followers went on spreading his ideas long after his death in 1542.

EXPLORING THE BODY

Other Renaissance thinkers explored the structure of the human body in detail for the first time. Artists, especially in northern Italy, led the way. They were already in the same guild as physicians and apothecaries (drugmakers) because the tools of all these trades—mixtures and potions—seemed to be similar. Artists and physicians now found that they also shared an interest in anatomy. Renaissance artists such as Leonardo da Vinci wanted to paint and sculpt representations of humans exactly as they were. They felt that the only way they could learn the arrangement of body parts such as muscles was through dissecting dead human bodies.

The church no longer completely forbade human dissection, as it had done during most of the Middle Ages, but it certainly

Nights with the Dead

Famed Renaissance artist Leonardo da Vinci, like Galen, believed that dissecting dead bodies was essential for both artists and physicians. In this excerpt from his notebooks, reprinted in Roberto Margotta's History of Medicine, *Leonardo explains why and describes his own experience with dissection.*

"You who say that it is better to watch an anatomical demonstration than to see these drawings, you would be right if it were possible to observe all the details shown in such drawings on a single figure, in which with all your cleverness you will not see or acquire knowledge of more than some few veins, while in order to obtain a true and complete knowledge of these, I have dissected more than ten human bodies, destroying all the various members and removing the minutest particles of flesh which surrounded these veins, without causing any effusion [outflow] of blood other than the imperceptible bleeding of the capillary [tiniest] veins. And as one single body did not suffice for so long a time, it was necessary to proceed by stages with so many bodies as would render my knowledge complete; this I repeated twice in order to discover the differences. And though you should have love for such things you may perhaps be deterred [kept away] by natural repugnance [disgust], and if this does not prevent you, you may perhaps be deterred by fear of passing the night hours in the company of these corpses, quartered [cut in four parts] and flayed [skinned] and horrible to behold; and if this does not deter you, then perhaps you may lack the skill in drawing . . . and the methods of estimating the force and strength of muscles; or perhaps you may be wanting [lacking] in patience so that you will not be diligent."

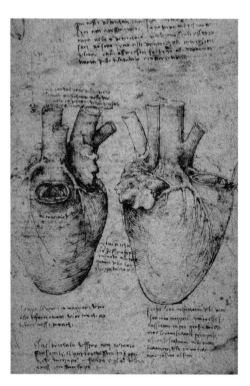

Renaissance artist Leonardo da Vinci's drawing of a human heart.

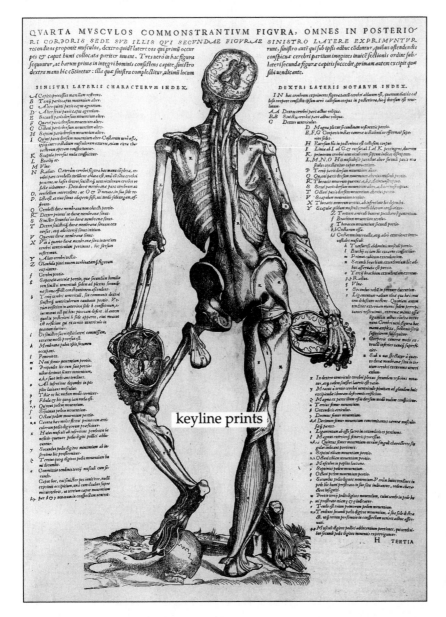

An engraving, probably by Jan van Calcar, in Vesalius's 1543 anatomy book On the Fabric of the Human Body *shows a cadaver's bones and muscles.*

did not encourage the practice. Fearing the church's displeasure, Leonardo, for example, did his dissections at night and probably in secret. He hid the hundreds of beautiful anatomical drawings he made in the early 1500s. They were published only in the late eighteenth century.

Physicians also began studying anatomy. The leader in this part of Renaissance medicine's rebirth was Andreas van Wesele, or Vesalius. Born in Brussels, in what is now Belgium, in 1514, Vesalius studied medicine at the University of Paris. Watching one or two dissections a year with a crowd of other medical students was not enough for Versalius. He stole the corpse of a hanged criminal from a roadside gallows, took it back to his room, and dissected it himself.

As soon as Vesalius finished medical school in 1537, the prestigious University of Padua in Italy hired him to teach anatomy to its students. He told them that his dissections had revealed a shocking fact: The all-but-sacred Galen, in guessing about human anatomy based on dissections of animals, had made serious mistakes. Vesalius wrote,

> How much has been attributed to Galen, easily leader of the professors of dissection, by those physicians and anatomists who have followed him, and often against reason! . . . Indeed, I myself cannot wonder enough at my own stupidity and too great trust in the writings of Galen and other anatomists.[18]

In 1543, when he was just twenty-eight years old, Vesalius published a detailed description of human anatomy in a book titled *On the Fabric of the Human Body*. This book pictured and described bones, muscles, blood vessels, nerves, and internal organs. It also showed how these parts of the body related to each other. Artist Jan van Calcar, who had worked with Vesalius before, probably made the book's fine drawings.

Vesalius's work was by far the most accurate anatomy text made up to that time. It summed up the growing Renaissance feeling that understanding the body's structure and function was vital to medi-

cine. Vesalius's fellow professors, however, criticized him severely for daring to question the teachings of Galen. Powerful figures in the church also were not pleased. Fearing prison or worse, Vesalius burned all of his unpublished work and left Padua. He later became a physician in the courts of two European rulers. He never wrote another book, but his anatomy text inspired many other researchers. Thanks to Vesalius and those who followed him, the study of anatomy became a regular part of medical training.

GENTLER SURGERY

Surgery might have seemed likely to gain from the Renaissance's discoveries about anatomy. That did not happen, however, perhaps because few surgeons actually studied anatomy in medical schools, but instead learned their craft from other surgeons. Still, surgeons were responsible for some major advances in medicine. One such pioneer was a French surgeon named Ambroise Paré. Chiefly an army surgeon, Paré proved the truth of the old Hippocratic saying that "He who desires to practice surgery must go to war."[19]

Paré invented several ways to make surgery more effective and less damaging for his patients. He found, for instance, that treating the wounds of soldiers injured by the newly developed gunpowder weapons with an ointment helped them heal much better than the standard procedure of scalding the wound with boiling oil. He also developed the technique of tying blood vessels shut after amputations

Sixteenth-century French surgeon Ambroise Paré's innovations made surgery a less dangerous procedure.

New Epidemics

The battle wounds Paré treated were fearsome, but contagious diseases such as smallpox and measles killed far more soldiers in crowded military camps. Such diseases took an even larger toll on civilians. Bubonic plague, for example, swept through Europe time and again. Britain had plague epidemics in 1563, 1603, 1625, and 1665. Each killed about a fifth of the people in London. In addition, a seemingly new disease called syphilis became widespread in the sixteenth century. Disfiguring, deadly, and spread through sex, this illness frightened people and caused many to condemn those who suffered from it.

Sixteenth-century doctors had no more luck in treating these diseases than physicians had had in treating the plague during the days of the Black Death. Indeed, although Renaissance discoveries in medical science were important for later researchers, they had little effect on most parts of medicine during their own time. As British philosopher Francis Bacon noted around the end of the sixteenth century, "Medicine is a science which hath been . . . more professed [talked about] than laboured, and yet more laboured than advanced; the labour having been, in my judgement, rather in circle than in progression. For I find much iteration [repetition], but small addition."[21]

rather than burning the wound to prevent bleeding. Unlike Galen and Paracelsus, Paré was modest about his accomplishments. He often said of his patients, "I dressed him [covered and cared for his wounds] and God healed him."[20] In the 1560s and 1570s he wrote several huge books about surgery that became standard references for many years. He also became a respected statesman and the court surgeon for four French kings.

3 Medicine Becomes a Science

In the seventeenth century scientific thinking went through a revolution. As a result, Europeans' view of the universe and their place in it changed completely. People had already been shocked in the Renaissance when Nicolaus Copernicus proved that the earth revolved around the sun. That meant that the earth and its human cargo were not the center of the universe, as everyone had thought. In the new century Galileo Galilei added to the shock by finding new moons and planets in the solar system. Isaac Newton showed that simple mathematical rules governed gravity and other forces in physics. And Robert Boyle, through his works, began to change the mystical art of alchemy into the science of chemistry.

Thinkers of this time revived and extended the scientific method that Aristotle had developed. They observed, measured, and experimented. They divided natural phenomena into parts—dissected them, in a sense—to learn how they worked. They tried to find a small number of simple, basic rules that would explain how all living and nonliving things behaved. They began meeting in scientific societies, such as the Royal Society in England and the Academy of Sciences in France, to describe and discuss what they had learned.

Early in the seventeenth century the French philosopher René Descartes summed up the scientific views of his time. Nature, he claimed, was nothing more than matter in motion, following mathematical laws. He said that living things, including humans, were merely complex machines. He added, however, that humans were special because they had souls.

BLOOD MOVES IN A CIRCLE

Physicians such as the Englishman William Harvey applied this new scientific approach to the study of anatomy. Born in the coastal town of Folkestone in 1578, Harvey studied medicine at Cambridge University in Britain and then in Padua. After he returned to England, he became a prominent physician in London. He later was the personal doctor and friend of King Charles I. In his spare time he dissected animals to learn about the body. His special interest was the circulatory system.

Galen had said that there were two types of blood. Bright red blood was car-

William Harvey (1578–1657), an English physician and anatomist, developed a new theory on the circulation of blood.

ried in vessels (tubes) called arteries, while thicker, bluish blood flowed in other vesssels called veins. Pulsing in the vessel walls moved the blood along. Galen thought the liver made the blood in the veins, while the heart made the blood in the arteries. Both kinds of blood, he said, moved through the body only once and then were used up.

Harvey's dissections led him to propose a different system. The heart, he said, was a muscle. It pumped blood through the arteries, working much like the water pumps that were starting to be used in England. The right ventricle (lower chamber) of the heart pushed the bluish blood from the veins into the pulmonary artery, which took it to the lungs. The pulmonary vein carried the blood, now somehow changed from blue to red, back to the left side of the heart. The left ventricle then pumped it out into the body through a giant artery called the aorta.

The blood, Harvey said, traveled through the body in smaller and smaller arteries. Finally, instead of being used up, it made its way into the veins, which brought it back to the heart. (Fabricius, Harvey's anatomy teacher in Padua, had shown him that the veins contained valves, like tiny swinging doors, which opened in just one direction. They forced the blood to flow toward the heart.) Thus, the blood moved through the body, over and over, in a circle. In fact it traveled in two circles, a small one through the lungs and a larger one through the rest of the body.

Harvey published his ideas in a book called *An Anatomical Essay on the Motion of the Heart and Blood in Animals* in 1628. "The blood in the animal body is impelled [pushed] in a circle. . . . This is the act or function which the heart performs by means of its pulse,"[22] he wrote. He proved the truth of almost all his concepts through drawings and accounts of experiments. For instance, he showed that blood could not constantly be produced anew by measuring the amount of blood pushed out of a sheep's heart in half an hour of pumping. This amount, he said, was far greater than the volume of blood in the whole animal. The only thing he could not show was the connections between the arteries and the veins.

Earlier anatomists had suggested some of these same ideas, but only Harvey

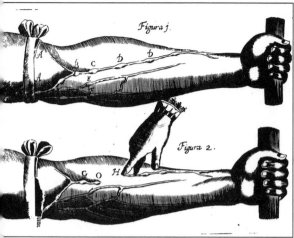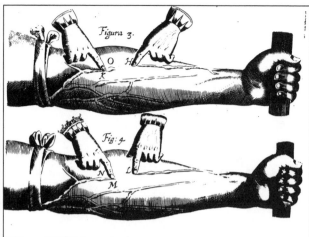

Illustrations from a book by William Harvey feature forearms with marked arteries to show that blood flows from the heart in a continuous cycle.

described the complete system of blood circulation and proved it by experiment. His work, like that of Vesalius, created a hot debate among physicians. Harvey wrote that his idea that the blood circulated throughout the body was "so . . . unheard-of that I not only fear injury to myself from the envy of a few, but I tremble lest I have mankind at large [as a whole] for my enemies"[23] because of it. Still, most physicians had accepted the idea by the time of Harvey's death in 1657. It marked as great a change in medical thinking as Copernicus's discovery had in astronomy.

UNDER THE MICROSCOPE

A new tool that Harvey did not use, although it existed in his time, helped scientists learn about the body in even more detail: the microscope. Invented by two Dutch spectacle (glasses) makers, Hans and Zacharias Janssen, around 1590, this new instrument used lenses (most often two or more, joined by a tube) to make objects look much larger than they really were. Like the telescope that Galileo used, the microscope greatly increased the range of observations that scientists could make.

Using a microscope, Marcello Malpighi, an Italian who taught medicine in Pisa and Bologna, found the parts of the blood circulation puzzle that had escaped Harvey. He discovered that arteries were linked with veins by tiny vessels called capillaries. Malpighi first saw capillaries in the lungs of a frog in 1661. He wrote,

> By the help of a glass [microscope] I saw not scattered points [spots of blood] but vessels joined together in a ring-like fashion. . . . They proceed from the vein on this [one] side and the artery on the other. . . . They do not keep a straight path but appear to form a network joining the two vessels. Thus it was clear that the blood

BLOOD MOVES IN A CIRCLE

"Since all things, both argument and ocular [visual] demonstration, show that the blood passes through the lungs and heart by the force of the ventricles [the heart's lower chambers], and is sent for distribution to all parts of the body, where it makes its way into the veins and porosities [tiny openings] of the flesh, and then flows by the veins from the circumference [outer parts of the body] on every side to the centre, from the lesser to the greater veins, and is by them finally discharged into the vena cava [the body's chief vein] and right auricle [upper chamber] of the heart, and this in such a quantity or in such a flux and reflux [flow forwards and backwards] thither by the arteries, hither by the veins, as cannot possibly be supplied by the ingesta [food that is eaten], and is much greater than can be required for mere purposes of nutrition [nourishing the body]; it is absolutely necessary to conclude that the blood in the animal body is impelled [moved] in a circle, and is in a state of ceaseless motion."

Seventeenth-century Italian physiologist Marcello Malpighi.

. . . did not empty into spaces, but was always contained within vessels, the paths of which produced its dispersion [spreading into the body].[24]

Malpighi also found that the lungs were made of soft, spongy material rather than being muscles, as had been thought. They were filled with thin-walled air pouches that hung like bunches of grapes from the ends of branching tubes. These tubes led back to the windpipe, or trachea, which joined the lungs with the mouth. Like Descartes, Malpighi saw the body as a machine. "The mechanisms of our bodies are composed of strings, thread, beams, levers, cloth, flowing fluids, cisterns, ducts, filters, sieves, and other similar mechanisms,"[25] he wrote.

Malpighi's microscope, like most others, had two lenses, but an eccentric Dutchman named Antoni van Leeuwenhoek made equally important finds using microscopes with only a single lens. Leeuwenhoek sold cloth for a living in the city of Delft. As a hobby, he made tiny microscopes that gave accurate images at much higher magnification than other microscopes of his day. Standard compound (multiple-lens) microscopes of the time could enlarge objects by only about 10 times. Leeuwenhoek's single lenses, however, could magnify up to 270 times. He never revealed how he made such perfect lenses.

With childlike wonder, Leeuwenhoek studied every living thing, or part of a living thing, that he could get his hands on. He was the first person to see spermatazoa, the tadpolelike sex cells of male animals. He also traced insects through their life cycles, during which many changed

56   ANTONI van LEEUWENHOEKS

Fig: 3   Fig: 4

Wanneer nu een ofte meer dierkens uit het mannelijk-zaad van een dier, foo verre in de Baar-moeder is ofte zijn gekomen, dat defelve dat deel in de Baar-moeder hebben aangetroffen, dat bequaam is om het felve te voeden, ende tot foodanigen foort van 'fchepfel te brengen, als wat het lighaam daar het zaad van afgekomen is; foo kan het fonder eenig nadenken feer ligt, en-de in Weinig tijdts gefchieden, dat de ftaart of ftaarten van de gefeide dierkens komen af te vallen, of dat zy het gantfche vel en ftaart te gelijk verwiffelen, ende dit dus gefchied fijnde, foo heeft ofte behoud het fchepfel als dan een ey-ronde figuur; als Fig. 3. FGH. ofte Fig. 4. IKL. Ten anderen weeten wy dat de lighamen van alle dieren, nog in de Baar-moeder fijnde, foo digt in een gebogen leggen, dat die meeft na een ronde figuur hellen. Is dit nu in de dieren die tot foodanigen groote gekomen zijn omme gebaart te werden, foo is zulks ook fonder twijfel in foodanige kleine fchepfels, die wy met het oog niet konnen bekennen, die ik dan oordeele

This page from a publication by Antoni van Leeuwenhoek offers a microscopic view of the living and dead spermatozoa of a dog.

LIVELY LITTLE ANIMALS

In a letter to Britain's Royal Society, a group of renowned scientists, Dutch microscope maker Antoni van Leeuwenhoek described the microorganisms he saw in matter scraped from his teeth. Leeuwenhoek's letter, dated September 17, 1683, is quoted in René Dubos's The Unseen World, *a book about discoveries made through the microscope.*

"I . . . saw, with great wonder, that in the . . . [scraped] matter there were many very little living animalcules [microbes], very prettily a-moving. The biggest sort . . . had a very strong and swift motion, and shot through the water (or spittle [saliva]) like a pike [a kind of fish]. . . . These were most always few in number.

The second sort . . . oft-times spun round like a top, and every now and then took a [zigzag] course . . . and these were far more in number.

The third sort . . . at times . . . seemed to be oblong [shaped like a flattened circle] while anon [at other times] they looked perfectly round. . . . They went ahead so nimbly, and hovered so together, that you might imagine them to be a big swarm of gnats or flies, flying in and out among one another."

their form greatly. Through his observations he proved that insects came from parents like themselves rather than arising from decaying matter, as many people then believed. Perhaps most important, in 1676 he found "little animals" in pond water and in scrapings from his own teeth. Some "leap[ed] about in the fluid like the fish called a jack," while others moved "with a whirling motion."[26] These were bacteria and other microorganisms. No one had ever seen them before.

ENLIGHTENMENT

Leeuwenhoek continued his observations into the eighteenth century, a time of po-

litical and social upheavals. This was a time when people in the Western world were looking toward new beginnings. Thinkers began to see history as "progress" rather than an endless series of cycles. They came to believe that, just as animals had developed from simple forms to more complex ones (which were seen as better) over time, humanity was learning more about the world and slowly making society better. Because they felt that their knowledge was so much greater than that of earlier times, they called this period the Enlightenment.

The key to future progress, Enlightenment thinkers believed, was science. Most educated Europeans agreed that observing, experimenting, and measuring were

An engraving in a 1793 book by Luigi Galvani shows the legs of dissected frogs and various devices used to measure what was thought to be electricity flowing in animals.

the best ways to learn about the world. They hoped to use science to control nature and help humanity. Many also wanted to apply scientific principles to social issues such as public health.

PHYSICS AND CHEMISTRY IN THE BODY

The great strides made in physics and chemistry in the seventeenth and eighteenth centuries led some researchers to use these sciences in studying the human body. Indeed, some thought all body functions could be explained by physics and chemistry. They saw no real difference between living and nonliving things. Other thinkers, however, claimed that a "vital spark" not explained by science gave living things unique features.

Some eighteenth-century scientists thought this vital spark might be just that: a form of electricity. Albrecht von Haller, a Swiss researcher, showed that all muscles have the power to contract (shrink or pull together), and all nerves have the

power to respond to signals. Two Italian scientists, Luigi Galvani and Alessandro Volta, did experiments whose results suggested that electricity might lie behind these qualities. For instance, they showed that passing an electric current through the nerves of a dead frog's leg made the muscles of the leg contract, just as if the frog were alive.

Some of the biggest discoveries in which chemistry and physics were applied to the body concerned respiration. British chemist Robert Boyle had shown in 1660 that candle flames went out and animals stopped breathing if they were deprived of air. This proved that air was required for both combustion (burning) and respiration. Jan Baptista van Helmont found that air was not a single substance but a mixture of gases. An English scientist, Joseph Priestley, and a German one, Karl Scheele, independently isolated the gas within air on which combustion and respiration depended. French chemist Antoine Lavoisier named the gas oxygen.

Lavoisier did many experiments on respiration. He showed it to be a process in which oxygen was taken into the body and two other gases, carbon dioxide and water vapor, were given off. His experiments proved that respiration and combustion were related. In 1783 he wrote,

> Respiration is . . . a combustion. . . . [It is] very slow. . . . Otherwise [it is] perfectly similar to that of . . . [charcoal]. It takes place in . . . the lungs. . . . The heat evolved [produced] . . . spreads into the blood which traverses [passes through] the lungs. . . . From there it is distributed through the whole animal system.[27]

By the end of the century scientists agreed that in respiration, oxygen from the air combined with carbon in food. The process produced heat and other forms of energy needed for life.

Eighteenth-century French chemist Antoine Lavoisier determined that respiration consisted of inhaling oxygen and exhaling carbon dioxide and water vapor.

French physiologist and anatomist Xavier Bichat (1771–1802) isolated twenty-one different types of body tissues.

THE EFFECTS OF DISEASE

Instead of studying the way healthy bodies worked, some scientists in the late eighteenth century looked at the ways bodies changed when they became diseased. The most important of these scientists was Giovanni Morgagni, who taught at the famous medical school in Padua, Italy. He performed hundreds of autopsies, or dissections done to find out the cause of death or damage done by disease. His book *On the Sites and Causes of Diseases*, published in 1761, matched signs of illness seen during life with physical changes visible after death. Morgagni helped to found the science of pathology, which studies changes that diseases make in the body.

Around the end of the century, a French scientist named Xavier Bichat revised

Morgagni's approach to pathology. Studying parts of the body under a microscope, Bichat focused on what he called tissues rather than on organs such as the heart or lungs. Tissues are structures that have features such as texture in common. The same tissue may appear in a number of different organs. Bichat identified twenty-one types of tissue in the human body, including muscle, nerve, and connective tissues.

TWO NEW DRUGS

Like the discoveries made during the Renaissance, most scientific advances in the seventeenth and eighteenth centuries had little effect on the day-to-day practice of medicine. British anatomist and physician Matthew Baillie admitted late in the eighteenth century, "I know better perhaps than another man, from my knowledge of anatomy, how to discover [identify] disease, but when I have done so, I don't know better how to cure it."[28]

In fact, only two really useful drugs were introduced during this time. One was cinchona bark, which came from a plant in Peru. First brought to Europe around 1633, it was sometimes called Jesuits' bark because the Jesuits, an order of Roman Catholic clerics, had an exclusive right to import it. Cinchona bark contains a substance, later called quinine, that destroys the microscopic organisms that cause malaria, a blood disease that produces repeated fevers, weakness, and sometimes death.

Cinchona bark was perhaps the first substance found to cure a specific disease.

Besides providing relief from a common and serious illness, it was important because it cast doubt on the Greek theory of humors, which many doctors still believed. If all fever was caused by an imbalance of humors, there was no reason why a medicine should cure one kind of fever but not others, as cinchona bark did.

The other useful medicine was digitalis, made from a common flowering plant called the foxglove. For centuries folk healers in England had used foxglove tea to treat dropsy, a swelling of the body caused by several kinds of illness. An English minister, William Withering, purified this substance in the early 1780s. He wrote that he had first heard of it as part of an herbal remedy "kept a secret by an old woman in Shropshire who had sometimes made cures [of dropsy with it] after the more regular practitioners had failed."[29] Withering also recognized that dried foxglove leaves had powerful effects on the heart. He warned, though, that it could be poisonous unless given in carefully measured, slowly increasing doses. The importance of Withering's discovery is illustrated by the fact that digitalis is still used to treat some kinds of heart disease.

"GO TO THE BEDSIDE"

The best physicians of the era followed Hippocrates' advice to pay close attention to their patients. These doctors included Thomas Sydenham in Britain in the early part of the seventeenth century and Hermann Boerhaave in Holland about fifty years later. Sydenham, whom admiring

English physician Thomas Sydenham advocated that doctors "go to the bedside" to get first-hand observations of a patient's illness.

fellow physicians called "the English Hippocrates," distrusted the new scientists' focus on dissection. He preferred to describe diseases as they appeared in living patients. On the other hand, Boerhaave, a renowned professor of medicine at the University of Leiden, made his students attend frequent autopsies. Both men agreed, though, that medical students' most important lessons came from seeing patients. "You must go to the bedside, it is there alone you can learn disease,"[30] Sydenham told one student. Boerhaave took his students through the wards of a local hospital and had them watch as he examined patients and discussed their illnesses.

Thanks to doctors like Sydenham and Boerhaave, work in hospitals became a standard part of physicians' training. John Aiken, a medical student in Scotland in the 1770s, described a typical hospital scene:

> A number of such cases [of disease] as are likely to prove instructive are selected and disposed [placed] in separate rooms in the Infirmary, and attended by one of the college professors. The students go round with him every day, and mark down the state of each patient and the medicines prescribed. At certain times lectures are read upon these cases.[31]

DOUBTFUL DOCTORS

Most doctors, however, did not have exceptional anatomical knowledge like Matthew Baillie, and they did not have the hospital experience that those who studied under Sydenham or Boerhaave had. They still memorized Galen and thought that disease was caused by imbalances in the four humors. They treated their patients mostly by bleeding and purging (giving treatments to empty the bowels), just as their forebears had done for centuries. Some still prescribed theriac. The luckiest patients had doctors who merely sent them to resorts such as Bath in England, where bathing in or drinking the local water was supposed to improve one's health.

Given physicians' ineffective and sometimes brutal treatments, it was not surprising that many people distrusted doctors. Writers such as the playwright Jean-Baptiste Molière and the philosopher François-Marie Voltaire made fun of high-society doctors' conceit and trickery. Ordinary people, most of whom could not have afforded a physician anyway, relied on local healers or traveling medicine sellers instead.

Some alternative healers offered gentler treatments than regular physicians. Others, however, had more dangerous tricks. They claimed to be able to cure any disease, but their potions gained most of their effects from alcohol or the narcotic opium. These false doctors came to be known as quacks. This term may have come from the Dutch word *quacksalver*, meaning quicksilver, or mercury, because some put compounds of this poisonous metal in their medicines. Blaming them for doing so seems unfair, though, because "legitimate" doctors used mercury too.

Despite their general failure to actually cure disease, doctors continued to search for more effective weapons against illness. The discovery in this period with the greatest real effect on medicine came at the end of the eighteenth century. Smallpox, a contagious disease now known to be caused by a virus, had terrorized most of the

---

FOOLISH PHYSICIANS

In this dialogue from a play called Love's the Best Doctor, *seventeenth-century French playwright Molière makes fun of foolish and sometimes dangerous high-society physicians. The passage, translated by H. Baker and J. Miller in 1739, is quoted in Logan Clendening's* Source Book of Medical History.

"*Lysetta.* What will you do, sir, with four physicians? Is not one enough to kill any one body?

Sganarel. Hold your tongue. Four advices are better than one.

Lysetta. Why, can't your daughter die well enough without the assistance of these gentlemen?

Sganarel. Do the physicians kill people?

Lysetta. Undoubtedly; and I knew a man who proved by good reasons that we should never say, such a one is dead [because] of a fever, or a catarrh [lung ailment], but she is dead of four physicians and two apothecaries [druggists].

Sganarel. Hush! Don't offend these gentlemen.

Lysetta. Faith, sir, our cat is lately recovered of a fall she had from the top of the house into the street, and was three days without either eating or moving foot or paw; but 'tis very lucky for her that there are no cat-doctors, for 'twould have been over with her [she would have died]. . . . They would not have failed purging her [giving her treatments to empty her bowels] and bleeding her.

Sganarel. Will you hold your tongue [be quiet], I say? What impertinence [disrespect] is this! Here they come.

Lysetta. Take care. You are going to be greatly edified [enlightened]; they'll tell you in Latin that your daughter is sick."

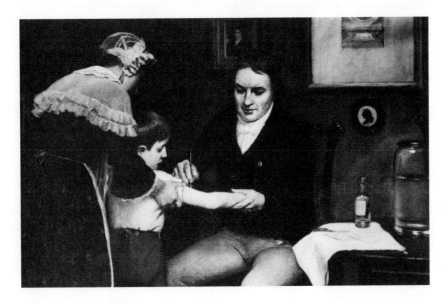

Dr. Edward Jenner vaccinates eight-year-old James Phipps on May 14, 1796. The vaccination proved successful and the boy did not develop smallpox.

world since ancient times. It caused some 60 million deaths in Europe during the eighteenth century alone. Those who survived it were often left with hideous scars from its oozing rash. People in a number of cultures, however, had noticed that survivors never caught the disease again. They found that they could protect themselves against serious attacks of the illness by scratching matter from smallpox sores into their skin, thereby giving themselves what was usually a mild case of the disease. This practice, called variolation, was brought to England in the early eighteenth century. Unfortunately, it sometimes produced full-blown cases of smallpox.

An English country doctor named Edward Jenner heard about variolation. He also learned from his village patients a common belief that dairymaids who caught cowpox from the cows they milked never developed smallpox. Cowpox was much like smallpox but was always a mild illness. Jenner therefore thought he might

be able to use matter from cowpox sores to produce the same result as variolation but with less risk. On May 14, 1796, he scratched matter from a dairymaid's cowpox sore into the arm of an eight-year-old boy named James Phipps. Six weeks later he scratched smallpox matter into the boy's arm as a test. Phipps did not develop smallpox.

After trying his procedure on twenty-three other people, Jenner published an account of his work in 1798. His technique became known as vaccination, after *vaccinia*, the Latin name for cowpox. The procedure quickly became popular throughout Europe. More than five thousand people had been vaccinated in England alone by 1799. Vaccination prevented many deaths and much disfigurement from smallpox. Jenner's success, perhaps more than anything else in the seventeenth and eighteenth centuries, showed what the scientific method could do for medicine and foreshadowed victories to come.

4 Invisible Enemies

Western society changed dramatically in the nineteenth century. So did medicine, especially in understanding epidemic diseases. For just about the first time in history, physicians became able to prevent a number of these mass killers.

The change in society was called the industrial revolution. It began in Britain in the late eighteenth century and spread during the next century to other parts of Europe and North America. The term *industrial revolution* referred to the fact that the steam engine (invented in the early 1770s) and the devices it powered, such as spinning and weaving machines, completely altered the way people worked. Instead of laboring at home or in small shops with just a few employees, many people found themselves working in factories alongside dozens or even hundreds of others. Factories clustered in places that had water or other sources of power for their machinery, and cities grew up or expanded around them. The promise of jobs drew people from the countryside into the cities, and a rise in total population made the crowding in cities even worse.

Life in the cities may have offered jobs, but to many people it provided little else. Workers in the new factories were often poorly paid, poorly fed, and made to labor under terrible circumstances. At home they crowded together in appalling conditions, surrounded by garbage heaps that included dead animals and human waste.

"HOLLOW-EYED GHOSTS"

Surroundings like these threatened people's health in countless ways. Some people suffered from diseases such as rickets, caused by the lack of calcium and phosphorus in their diet. Others had work-related illnesses such as miners' "black lung," an illness caused by constantly inhaling coal dust. Worst of all, epidemic diseases struck hardest among the poor. Friedrich Engels, a factory owner in Manchester, England, who later became a follower of Communist thinker Karl Marx, called that city's slum dwellers "pale, lank, narrow-chested, hollow-eyed ghosts."[32]

Two contagious illnesses, one old and one new, made special attacks on nineteenth-century slums. The old one was tuberculosis, which came to be called the "white plague" perhaps because its victims looked pale and wasted. This disease had been known since ancient Egypt.

A slum in London, England, during the industrial revolution. The squalid living conditions in these areas allowed rickets, black lung, tuberculosis, and cholera to flourish.

It occurred during the nineteenth century to a greater extent than ever before, however, because of overcrowding and poor nutrition. "No other [disease] is so common,"[33] one observer wrote at the start of the century, and it became even more so by the end.

The new disease—new to the West, at least—was cholera. Cholera caused vomiting and diarrhea so severe that it killed most of its victims through dehydration. Cholera had existed in India since early times, but it came to Europe only after Europeans began trading with India regularly. The first cholera pandemic (worldwide epidemic) to reach Europe and North America appeared in 1832. Others followed in 1852 and 1863.

Eighteenth-century thinkers had noticed links between epidemics, poverty, and filth. Poor people's dirty, foul-smelling surroundings were thought to create the "bad air" that many physicians believed was the cause of epidemics. Reformers in the

A Cry for Help

Not only physicians and government officials understood that unclean, poor environments spread disease. This badly spelled but touching appeal written by someone living in such a community demonstrates that poor people were also aware of the health threats posed by their surroundings. This letter, printed in the London Times *during the cholera epidemic of 1849, is quoted in Roy Porter's* The Greatest Benefit to Mankind.

"Sur,

May we be and beseach [beg] your proteckshion and power. We are Sur, as it may be, livin in a Wilderness, so far as the rest of London knows anything of us, or as the rich and great people care about. We live in muck and filth. We aint got no priviz [toilets], no dust bins, no drains, no watersplies [supplies], and no drain or suer [sewer] in the hole place. The Suer Company, in Greek St., Soho Square, all great, rich powerfool men take no notice watsomdever of our complaints. The Stenche [smell] of a Gulley-hole [cesspool] is disgustin. We all of us suffer, and numbers are ill, and if the Cholera comes Lord help us."

---

nineteenth century studied this connection more closely. They began taking steps to break the chain that brought early death to so many workers and their families.

One of the chief health reformers in Britain was Edwin Chadwick. Working for the British government, he and other researchers visited poor neighborhoods and studied data about citizens such as records of births and deaths, which the government had begun to collect in the seventeenth century. They then produced a massive document in 1842 titled *Report on the Sanitary Condition of the Labouring Population of Great Britain*. The report concluded that the widespread sickness among poor people was caused by their unsanitary surroundings. The conditions described in Chadwick's report were so terrible that one observer said government leaders read them "with astonishment, dismay, horror and even incredulity [disbelief]."[34]

Chadwick's group believed that much of this illness could be prevented by cleaning up these surroundings. They wrote,

> The primary and most important measures, and at the same time the most practicable, and within the recognized province of administration, are drainage, the removal of all refuse [garbage] from habitations [homes], streets and roads, and the improvement of the supplies of water.[35]

The government was slow to act on Chadwick's advice, partly because his claim of a link between filth and disease was not very precise. By the middle of the century, however, a London physician named John Snow was able to make the connection much clearer in the case of cholera. Because cholera chiefly affected the digestive system, Snow thought it was likely to be spread through food or water. He especially suspected drinking water as being the culprit. He had many chances to test his theory during cholera epidemics in the city in 1849 and 1854.

Snow found some of his best evidence in a severe outbreak that occurred in early September 1854 in a tiny London neighborhood called Golden Square. More than five hundred people died of cholera in this neighborhood within ten days. Snow later called it "the most terrible outbreak of cholera which ever occurred in this kingdom."[36]

Nineteenth-century English reformer Edwin Chadwick stated that the illnesses plaguing the poor resulted from an unsanitary environment.

Golden Square centered on Broad Street, which contained a well from which many residents pumped their drinking water. Snow found that fifty-nine of the seventy-seven cholera-stricken households about which he could gather information took their drinking water from this source. Most households that remained healthy, however, got their water elsewhere. He strongly suspected that the well had become contaminated with matter from a nearby cesspool that contained human and household wastes.

Snow explained his ideas to the Board of Guardians of St. James's Parish, the closest thing to a local government that the area had, on September 7. He begged them to have the handle of the pump on the Broad Street well removed so that people could no longer use the well. According to Edwin Lankester, a local physician, "not a member of his own profession, not an individual in the parish believed Snow was right."[37] Still, the board was desperate to stop the sickness, so it agreed to his request. The outbreak ended very shortly thereafter.

The Golden Square cholera outbreak had already been declining and probably would have stopped soon in any case. However, later investigation suggested that Snow's action saved lives by keeping new outbreaks from arising at the same spot. As Snow had guessed, the bricks between the cesspool and the well on Broad Street turned out to be old and broken. Stains traced an underground path between the two, proving that the cesspool's contents had leaked into the well water. An account in the book *Epidemic!* written to accompany a 1999 American Museum of Natural History exhibit that described the investigation of epidemic disease, says that Snow's disabling of the Broad Street pump "was the first reported instance of direct action to end a public health menace based on scientifically gathered . . . data."[38]

Snow published his evidence that drinking water spread cholera in an 1849 book called *On the Mode of Communication of Cholera*, which he revised in 1855. This publication convinced at least a few officials that providing pure drinking water could help to prevent cholera and perhaps

other epidemic diseases. Thanks to research like Snow's, Britain and, later, other European countries and the United States took steps to clean up unsanitary environments and safeguard public health.

INVISIBLE KILLERS

A little more than ten years later, an English surgeon named Joseph Lister went even further than Snow in preventing disease. Working at a hospital in Glasgow, Scotland, Lister was deeply disturbed by

---

CONVICTING THE BROAD STREET PUMP

In his 1855 revision of On the Mode of Communication of Cholera, *physician John Snow gives examples to support his belief that cholera in one part of London was being spread through contaminated drinking water pumped from a well on Broad Street. Logan Clendening's* Source Book of Medical History *reprints this passage from Snow's book.*

"The Workhouse [government institution to house the poor and homeless] in Poland Street is more than three-fourths surrounded by houses in which deaths from cholera occurred, yet out of five hundred and thirty-five inmates only five died of cholera. . . . The workhouse has a pump-well on the premises, in addition to the supply from the Grand Junction Water Works, and the inmates never sent to Broad Street for water. . . .

Mr. Marshall, surgeon, . . . was kind enough to inquire respecting [regarding] seven workmen who had been employed . . . at Nos. 8 and 9 Broad Street, and who died in their homes. He learned that they were all in the habit of drinking water from the pump, generally drinking about half-a-pint once or twice a day; while two persons who reside constantly on the premises, but do not drink the pump-water, only had diarrhoea. Mr. Marshall also informed me of the case of an officer in the army, who lived at St. John's Wood, but came to dine in Wardour Street, where he drank the water from Broad Street pump at his dinner. He was attacked with cholera, and died in a few hours."

English surgeon Joseph Lister (1827–1912) discovered antiseptics, substances that prevent infection in wounds.

the fact that so many of his patients died from infections that began in wounds and then spread through their bodies. He knew this happened in every other hospital, too. Almost half of all patients whose arms or legs had to be amputated, for example, died of infection. In fact, infection of wounds was so common that historically many doctors—starting with Galen —had thought it was a normal and even desirable part of healing.

Some other surgeons of Lister's time shared his distress over the deaths due to infection. One said that infection was more deadly even than war. People going to a hospital for surgery were "exposed to more chances of death than was the English sol-

dier on the field of Waterloo [a famous battle between France and England in 1815]."[39] Few doctors saw any link between the high rate of infection and their own actions, however. Most wore the same blood-caked clothes day after day while they performed their operations. They might wash their hands or instruments when they were through seeing patients, but they saw no reason to do so before they started. Infection, they thought, was surely caused by the foul-smelling air that gathered in the hospital wards.

Lister had a more open mind about what might cause infection. In 1864 he was amazed to read that a French chemist, Louis Pasteur, had recently shown that the air was full of living things so small that they could be seen only with a microscope. Some of these microscopic organisms caused fermentation, a process that broke down sugars in plant and animal products to form substances such as alcohol. Other organisms caused putrefaction, a related process that decayed meat or other animal matter. After learning about what he called "the beautiful researches of Pasteur,"[40] Lister realized that wound infections were much like decay except that they took place in living bodies. He decided that microorganisms (sometimes called microbes or germs) might cause wound infections as well as putrefaction.

PROTECTING WOUNDS

If microbes caused wound infections, Lister reasoned, he should be able to prevent the infections by killing microbes in wounds

A Careless Surgeon

Except for its last detail, this passage, quoted in Roy Porter's The Greatest Benefit to Mankind, *could have been written about almost any nineteenth-century surgeon in the days before Joseph Lister created his system of antisepsis to protect patients against infection. Disturbingly, however, the passage, written by surgeon Berkeley Moynihan, describes a surgeon in the British city of Leeds in 1880, almost fifteen years after Lister's system was introduced.*

"He rolled up his shirt-sleeves and, in the corridor to the operation room, took an ancient frock [long coat] from a cupboard; it bore signs of a checquered [mixed] past, and was utterly stiff with old blood. One of these coats was worn with special pride, indeed joy, as it had belonged to a retired member of the staff. The cuffs were rolled up to only just above the wrists, and the hands were washed in a sink. Once clean (by conventional standards), they were rinsed in carbolic-acid solution."

and keeping others from entering. He read about a powerful chemical called carbolic acid, which officials of one Scottish town had poured on sewage used as fertilizer to keep it from causing disease. Carbolic acid could burn the skin, but Lister hoped that if he mixed it with water, he could use it to kill microbes in wounds without harming healthy tissue too much.

Lister first tried his carbolic acid treatment on August 12, 1865. His patient was an eleven-year-old boy named James Greenlees, whose leg had been broken when a cart ran over it. One end of the broken bone had pushed through the skin of the leg, a condition called a compound fracture. The wounds produced by compound fractures almost always became infected. After Lister covered Greenlees's wound with cloth soaked in carbolic acid, however, it healed without infection.

Lister used his treatment on other compound fracture patients with equal success. He published his results in the March 16, 1867, issue of the British medical journal *Lancet*. After making further tests, he described his technique in more detail in a longer paper later that same year. He called his procedure antisepsis, which means "against infection." He wrote,

Since the antiseptic treatment has been brought into full operation, and wounds and abscesses no longer poison the atmosphere with putrid exhalations [gas that smells of decay], my wards, though in other respects under precisely the same circumstances as before, have completely changed their character; so that during the last nine months not a single instance of pyaemia, hospital gangrene, or erysipelas [different types of wound infection] has occurred in them.[41]

Lister eventually brought antisepsis into the operating room. He advised surgeons to wash their hands, their instruments, and even the walls and floor of the room in a carbolic acid solution before operating. During his own surgeries, he had a mist containing carbolic acid sprayed in the room to kill microbes in the air.

At first, British surgeons were not eager to adopt Lister's methods. They disliked working with the carbolic acid, which irritated their skin. They had never heard of Pasteur or, if they had, they questioned his results. These doctors had trouble believing that living things too small for them to see could cause fatal illnesses. They also hated to think that they themselves were spreaders of disease and death. Lister, however, kept calmly repeating his message. In time, the success of his methods, which brought the death toll from his operations down to 2 percent, convinced other surgeons that he was right.

Surgeons in Germany and France accepted Lister's approach more quickly than those in Britain. U.S. surgeons, on the other hand, were even slower than the British to take it up. By the end of the nineteenth century, however, antisepsis was saving lives almost everywhere. But as surgeons came to realize that microorganisms on hands and other surfaces were a greater threat than those in the air, Lister's

A cloth covered in chloroform is held over a patient's face while a carbolic acid spray creates an antiseptic atmosphere. Lister first used carbolic acid in 1865.

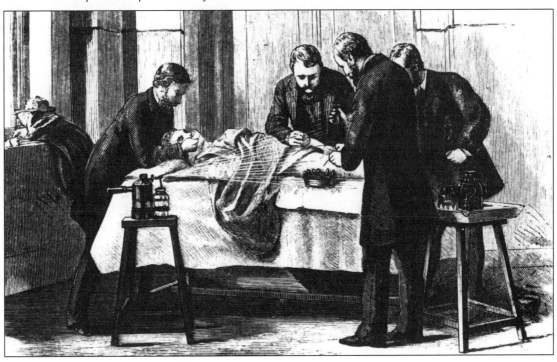

carbolic acid spray dropped out of use. (Even Lister gave it up in 1890.) Instead, many surgeons used protective clothing such as face masks and rubber gloves to keep microbes on their bodies from entering patients' wounds. This approach was called asepsis, or "no infection." One surgeon wrote in 1910,

> Operating theatres [rooms] which resembled shambles [butcher's shops] in 1860 are replaced by rooms of spotless purity containing . . . metal furniture and ingenious electric lights. All concerned in the operation are clothed from nose-tip to toe-tip in sterilised linen gowns, and their hands are covered with sterilised rubber gloves.[42]

PASTEUR'S GERM THEORY

While Lister was developing antisepsis and trying to persuade other surgeons to adopt it, the man who had inspired him, Louis Pasteur, was also exploring the idea that microorganisms could cause disease as well as infections in wounds. Since the days of the ancient Greeks, thinkers had proposed that contagious diseases were spread by some kind of invisible particles, which might be alive. No one, however, had been able to prove these particles' existence or say what they were. Few scientists had studied the "little animals" that Antoni van Leeuwenhoek had spotted more than a hundred years earlier because they were very hard to see until compound microscopes were improved in the 1830s. (One of the key improvements, in fact, had been made by Joseph Lister's father.) Pasteur's discovery that microbes caused fermentation and putrefaction, however, led him to link microorganisms with disease, just as Lister had.

Pasteur first showed in the late 1860s that a microbe caused a disease that was killing silkworms, a kind of caterpillar that was the basis of the French silkmaking industry. He then studied a number of infectious diseases that affected animals and humans. In most cases Pasteur either identified the microbe that caused the disease or confirmed the work of others who had done so. In key papers presented to the French Academy of Medicine in 1878, he described what came to be called the germ theory of disease. It stated that infectious diseases were caused by microorganisms that invaded the body and that different types of microbes caused different diseases. Some of the French doctors argued with him, but he had no patience with them. "I shall force them to see; they will have to see!"[43] he raged.

Pasteur also found ways to prevent some of these diseases. In 1854, for example, he showed that microbes causing undesirable fermentation in wine could be killed by heat treatment, a technique that came to be called pasteurization. This technique was later used on milk and other liquids to kill disease-causing microbes in them. The pasteurization of milk stopped one way in which tuberculosis was spread.

Furthermore, while studying a form of cholera that infected chickens, Pasteur found that allowing a culture (a colony of microorganisms grown in the laboratory) to age weakened the microbes in it. When these weakened germs were injected into a chicken, they failed to make the bird sick. Better still, chickens treated in this way remained healthy even when later injected with unweakened cholera germs. This effect was much like the one Edward Jenner had discovered for cowpox, and Pasteur called his technique vaccination in Jenner's honor. Instead of depending on the lucky discovery of a naturally weak form of a disease, however, Pasteur's approach involved weakening microorganisms on purpose in the laboratory. Using various methods, Pasteur made vaccines for several important diseases in the early 1880s. One was for anthrax, which caused great losses of French sheep and cattle and sometimes killed humans. Another was for rabies, an always-fatal brain disease sometimes spread to humans bitten by infected animals.

Nineteenth-century French chemist and biologist Louis Pasteur looks on as a patient receives a vaccination for rabies.

KOCH'S RULES

Meanwhile, a country doctor in Germany named Robert Koch was developing a sound scientific basis for the still-controversial theory that microorganisms caused disease. He built on the ideas of his teacher, Jacob Henle, who had written around 1840 that "the substance of contagion is not only organic but living."[44] Koch worked out basic rules, called Koch's postulates or the Koch-Henle postulates, that are still accepted as a means of demonstrating that a particular microbe causes a disease:

1. The microbe must be found in all animals or people with the disease.

2. The microbe can be taken from the body of a living thing with the disease and grown in a pure culture (one containing no other kind of microorganism) in the laboratory.

3. Injecting a pure culture of the microbe into a laboratory animal gives the animal the disease.

4. The microbe can be taken from this sick animal and grown in pure culture once more.

Koch published these postulates in a paper in 1882. In the paper he used them to prove that a certain kind of bacteria causes tuberculosis. He and his coworkers went on to identify the microbes that cause several other epidemic diseases, including human cholera in 1884. (He also

German physiologist Emil von Behring (1854–1917) in his lab with an assistant. Behring won the 1901 Nobel Prize for his work with diphtheria immunizations.

confirmed John Snow's guess that this disease is spread through drinking water.) Using Koch's postulates, in each year between 1879 and 1900, researchers discovered at least one microorganism that causes a major human disease.

A TRUE REVOLUTION

By the end of the nineteenth century, the work of Koch, Pasteur, and their followers had convinced nearly everyone that microorganisms caused many human illnesses, especially those that infected large numbers of people at once. This knowledge, in turn, helped scientists work out ways to prevent quite a few of the diseases, either by stopping their transmission or by creating vaccines against them.

Around 1890 a German researcher, Emil von Behring, and a Japanese coworker, Shibasaburo Kitasato, discovered a third way of fighting infectious disease. They found that injecting animals with small doses of certain disease-causing bacteria made the animals' serum, the liquid part

of the blood, develop the ability to fight the bacteria. Unlike a vaccine, this antiserum, as it came to be called, could help people who had already caught a disease. It cured them by destroying poisons, or toxins, that the bacteria made. The first antiserum was used to treat diphtheria, a major killer of children, in Berlin in 1891. French scientists then developed a way to make it on a large scale.

These new methods of prevention and treatment, combined with public health measures that made people's environments cleaner and improved their diets, led to a great reduction in deaths from epidemic diseases. As a result, both population and life expectancy rose in Europe and North America. Historian Roy Porter writes,

> The latter part of the nineteenth century brought one of medicine's few true revolutions. . . . The new disease theories [of Pasteur and Koch] led directly and rapidly to genuinely effective preventive measures and remedies, saving lives on a dramatic scale.[45]

Chapter

5 Journeys into the Body

While Pasteur, Koch, and others were proving that some diseases were caused by invisible invaders coming from outside the body, other researchers drew on new technology to probe deep into the body itself. Laboratory scientists used improved microscopes to study the cells of which all bodies are made. Physicians employed new devices to find out what was going on inside their patients. And aided by Lister's antisepsis and another nineteenth-century discovery, anesthesia, surgeons ventured into parts of the body they had never dared to operate on before.

BREAKING DOWN FOOD

Some laboratory researchers, especially in Germany, focused on chemical reactions that go on inside living things. They laid the foundation for what would become biochemistry. For example, Justus von Liebig, a professor at Munich University, studied the processes by which animals make energy from food. In doing so he added to the eighteenth-century research on respiration.

Far away in the United States another researcher seized a unique chance to study a related subject, the chemistry of digestion, in a living human being. William Beaumont, a U.S. army surgeon stationed at Fort Mackinac in northern Michigan, was called to treat a French-Canadian fur trapper named Alexis St. Martin one day in 1822. St. Martin had been shot in the abdomen by a musket, producing a terrible wound. To Beaumont's amazement, St. Martin survived. Furthermore, his wound healed almost completely—except for a permanent opening that led directly into the young man's stomach.

For years, Beaumont used St. Martin as a human guinea pig. He tied pieces of different foods to threads and inserted them into the man's stomach through the hole. After various lengths of time, he removed and examined them to find out how quickly they were digested. Beaumont showed that the stomach digested food by partly dissolving it, rather than by breaking it up or making it decay. He described his studies in a book called *Experiments and Observations on the Gastric [Stomach] Juice and the Physiology of Digestion*, published in 1833.

The nineteenth century's improved microscopes helped researchers who studied the structure and function of the body, just

Window into the Stomach

"August 1, 1825. At 12 o'clock M. [noon], I introduced through the perforation [hole], into the stomach, the following articles of diet, suspended by a silk string, and fastened at proper distances, so as to pass in without pain . . . : a piece of highly seasoned *a la mode beef*; a piece of *raw, salted, fat pork*; a piece of *raw, salted, lean beef*; a piece of *boiled, salted beef*; a piece of *stale bread*; and a bunch of *raw, sliced cabbage*; each piece weighing about two drachms; the lad continuing unusual employment about the house.

At 1 o'clock P.M., withdrew and examined them—found the *cabbage* and *bread* about half digested; the pieces of *meat* unchanged. Returned them into the stomach.

At 2 o'clock P.M., withdrew them again—found the *cabbage, bread, pork,* and *boiled beef,* all cleanly digested, and gone from the string; the other pieces of meat but very little affected. Returned them into the stomach again."

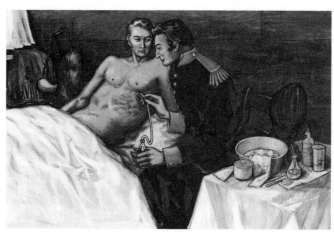

U.S. army surgeon William Beaumont inserts a tube into the stomach of Alexis St. Martin.

as they aided Pasteur and Koch by revealing the organisms that could infect a body. In 1839, after examining plant and animal tissues under the microscope, German scientists Matthias Schleiden and Theodor Schwann claimed that all living things were made up of units called cells. They took this name from the work of an earlier microscopist, Robert Hooke, who had used it in 1664 to describe the square, roomlike shapes he saw in a thin slice of wood. (Hooke in fact had not seen living cells, but the thick walls that remain in this kind of tissue after the cells have died.) Although cells in different types of body tissue appeared very different, Schleiden and Schwann pointed out, they had certain features in common. Each cell was surrounded by an outer membrane and contained a jellylike substance that came to be called cytoplasm. Most cells also had a central body called a nucleus.

Xavier Bichat's work in the eighteenth century had caused scientists' study of liv-

An illustration of animal and plant cells drawn by German scientist Theodor Schwann.

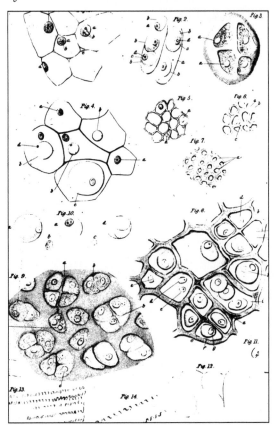

ing things to move from a focus on organs to one on tissues. In the nineteenth century, research zoomed in further to focus on cells. One of the chief researchers who studied the effects of disease on cells was another German, Rudolf Virchow. Virchow was a man of amazingly broad talents whose interests ranged from public health and politics to archaeology and history. His influence on medical research was so great that it was compared with the pope's influence in the Catholic Church.

Virchow agreed with Schleiden and Schwann that living things were made of cells. He called the body a "cellular democracy."[46] Some scientists, including Schwann, had thought that cells could be created out of unorganized matter within the body. Virchow showed, however, that cells were always produced by other cells. All the cells in a living thing's body, he said, could be traced back to the fertilized egg, the single cell formed when an egg and a sperm joined. In this research Virchow echoed proofs that Leeuwenhoek and others had made for insects and Pasteur had made for microbes. These scientists showed that living matter could not be created from nonliving matter. All living things, they taught, must have parents.

CELLS IN HEALTH AND DISEASE

Virchow went further by contending in *Cellular Pathology*, a famous book published in 1858, that all disease could be understood as problems within cells. He expressed doubt about the germ theory advanced by Pasteur and Koch, which saw disease as being caused by outside agents (microorganisms). In fact, both arguments were eventually proved partly right. Microorganisms can cause sickness, but they do so by damaging body cells. Other diseases, such as cancer, may result when cells are damaged by factors in the environment or become defective for unknown reasons.

Other researchers showed how cells work together to help the body function. French scientist Claude Bernard, for instance, proposed that cells in the bodies of warm-blooded animals, including humans, adjust the body's temperature, chemistry, and other factors to maintain a stable internal environment. This set of activities, which Bernard described in 1878, was later called homeostasis. It helps animals remain fairly independent of their environment. "The stability of the internal environment is the prime requirement for free, independent existence,"[47] Bernard wrote. Warm-blooded animals can move easily even in cold weather, for example, but cold-blooded animals such as insects and lizards cannot. The cold outside tem-

ALL CELLS COME FROM CELLS

Unlike some other researchers of his time, the highly respected German scientist Rudolf Virchow insisted that cells, the microscopic units making up the bodies of all living things, could not be created from nonliving matter. He explains this belief in this passage from his Cellular Pathology *(1858), translated in 1860 by Frank Chance and reprinted in* Source Book of Medical History, *edited by Logan Clendening.*

"Just as little as we can now admit that . . . out of the residue [remains] of the decomposition [breakdown] of animal or vegetable matter an infusorial animalcule, a fungus, or an alga [microorganisms], can be formed, equally little are we disposed to concede [admit] . . . that a new cell can build itself up out of any non-cellular substance. Where a cell arises, there a cell must have previously existed, just as an animal can spring only from an animal, a plant only from a plant. In this manner, although there are still a few spots in the body where absolute demonstration has not yet been afforded [made], the principle is nevertheless established, that in the whole series of living things, whether they be entire plants or animal organisms, or essential constituents [parts] of the same, an eternal law of continuous development prevails. There is no discontinuity of development of such a kind that a new generation can of itself give rise to a new series of developmental forms. No developed tissues can be traced back either to any large or small simple element, unless it be to a cell."

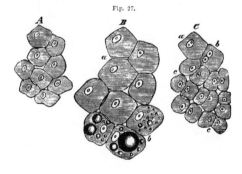
An engraving in Rudolf Virchow's 1858 Cellular Pathology *shows varying sizes of liver cells, illustrating Virchow's idea that disease alters cells.*

perature lowers the cold-blooded animals' body temperature so much that their
muscles do not work well.

Both Bernard and Virchow stressed that
physicians needed to understand how normal bodies work before they could understand the changes caused by disease.
"Disease is nothing but life under altered
conditions,"[48] Virchow said. Bernard wrote,
"Medicine is the science of sickness; physiology [the study of how bodies function] is
the science of life; thus physiology must be
the scientific basis of medicine."[49]

LISTENING TO THE HEART

While Virchow, Bernard, and other laboratory researchers were advancing the basic
science behind medicine, inventors were

creating tools that helped doctors find out what went on inside their patients. French physician René Laënnec developed the first of these devices in 1816. Before that time doctors trying to listen for signs of heart or lung disease had simply placed an ear on the patient's chest. Sometimes, they used a technique developed in the eighteenth century by an Austrian physician, Leopold Auenbrugger. The son of an innkeeper, Auenbrugger had learned as a child to thump a barrel of wine and use the resulting sound to judge how full the barrel was. He later found that tapping patients' chests with his finger produced equally useful information. A healthy chest sounded like a drum covered with cloth, he wrote. A muffled or high-pitched sound suggested lung problems.

Laënnec, however, found himself faced with a situation in which both these techniques were useless. His patient was a plump young woman who, he suspected, had heart disease. Social norms of the day forbade him from placing his head on the woman's chest, and tapping would not have produced useful sounds because she was so overweight. Seeking a way to listen to her heart in spite of these problems, Laënnec remembered seeing two boys playing. One boy had scratched one end of a wooden beam with a pin. The other had placed his ear on the other end of the beam to hear the sound, which carried clearly through the wood. The boys' game gave Laënnec an idea.

Since he didn't have a piece of wood, Laënnec rolled a sheaf of papers tightly into a tube. He placed one end on the young woman's chest near her heart and

French physician René Laënnec (1781–1826), inventor of the stethoscope. His first version of the device was paper rolled into a tube.

his ear next to the other end. To his delight, he found that the paper tube transmitted and magnified sound just as the wood had done. "I was both surprised and gratified at being able to hear the beating of the heart with much greater clearness and distinctness than I had ever before,"[50] he wrote later.

Laënnec described his invention, the stethoscope, in a lengthy book published in 1818. He explained how he had used the new instrument to identify lung diseases as well as heart problems. Laënnec made his stethoscopes out of wood. In 1852, however, an American physician named George P. Cammann created a better version of Laënnec's tool. Cammann's stethoscope had two earpieces and flexible tubing, much like the ones that doctors still use. Although stethoscopes became less important in the twentieth century, after X rays and other technology let physicians see into the body, they have remained useful tools. Indeed, the stethoscope has become a symbol of the physician.

Other devices followed the stethoscope. For instance, Hermann von Helmholtz, a German physician who specialized in studying the eye, developed the ophthalmoscope in 1851. This invention was a concave (inward-curving) mirror with a hole in the center. Looking through the hole from the back of the mirror, a doctor could see the inside of a patient's eye. Helmholtz described "the great joy of being the first to see a living human retina,"[51] the back of the inside of the eye.

LAËNNEC INVENTS THE STETHOSCOPE

In this passage, quoted in Roy Porter's Cambridge Illustrated History of Medicine, *French physician René Laënnec describes how he came to invent the stethoscope, a device that magnifies sounds coming from the chest.*

"In 1816 I was consulted by a young woman presenting general symptoms [signs] of disease of the heart. Owing to her stoutness little information could be gathered by application of the hand and percussion [tapping]. The patient's age and sex did not permit me to resort to [placing the ear on the chest]. . . . I recalled a well-known acoustic [sound] phenomenon, namely, if you place your ear against one end of a wooden beam the scratch of a pin at the other extremity [end] is distinctly audible. It occurred to me that this physical property might serve a useful purpose in the case with which I was then dealing. Taking a sheet of paper I rolled it into a very tight roll, one end of which I placed on the precordial region [the area above the heart], whilst I put my ear to the other. I was both surprised and gratified at being able to hear the beating of the heart with much greater clearness and distinctness than I had ever before by direct application of my ear.

I saw at once that this means might become a useful method for studying, not only the beating of the heart, but likewise all movements capable of producing sound in the thoracic vacity [chest cavity], and that consequently it might serve for the investigation of respiration [breathing], the voice, . . . and possibly even the movements of liquid effused into the pleural cavity [area around the lungs] or pericardium [sac surrounding the heart]."

Hermann Boerhaave and a few other eighteenth-century physicians had made taking patients' temperatures part of their hospital routine. Most doctors did not, however, because thermometers were a foot long and took twenty minutes to work. The situation changed when a Briton named Clifford Allbutt invented a practical thermometer in 1867. It was only about six inches long. Made of glass and filled with mercury, it displayed an accurate temperature after three minutes in a patient's mouth. It, too, soon became a standard instrument for every doctor.

Like the stethoscope and other new devices, Allbutt's improved thermometer gave physicians a precise way to detect and measure changes inside their patients' bodies. In doing so, these tools made clinical medicine more like a laboratory science. They made physicians' work more accurate, but they also sometimes distanced doctors from the people they treated. As a result of the growing emphasis on measurement and laboratory testing, one nineteenth-century German doctor complained, "The sick person has become a thing."[52]

AN END TO PAIN

Surgeons, meanwhile, were helped by another nineteenth-century innovation. Lister's antisepsis had removed (or at least greatly reduced) the threat of infection from surgical incisions, but pain during surgery made all but the simplest operations unbearable for the patient. Surgeons of earlier times had tried to deaden pain during operations with alcohol, opium, and a few other drugs. Until the mid-nineteenth century, however, patients understandably dreaded the surgeon's knife. (One surgeon recalled in 1848 that "a patient preparing for an operation was like a condemned criminal preparing for execution."[53])

The main thing a surgeon could do to make operations less painful was to be quick. One surgeon in the 1830s bragged that he could cut off a leg at the hip in ninety seconds, for example. A surgeon who was quick, however, could not be careful and thorough. Operations that could not be done quickly were all but impossible.

Anesthesia removed the threat of pain. An Austrian physician named Josef Weiger wrote in the mid-nineteenth century, shortly after anesthesia was introduced,

> This is the . . . greatest discovery of our century. I say the greatest discovery for, even though slowly, we could fulfil our other wishes though steamships and the electric telegraph had never been invented, [but] what will be gained by the prevention of pain in surgical operations can only be understood by those who have had to watch operations performed without anesthetics.[54]

The first step on the path to pain-free surgery was taken around 1800, when several young British men, including Humphry Davy (later a famous chemist), were experimenting with gases. Davy noticed that when he breathed one of these gases, nitrous oxide, he felt dizzy and giggly. Furthermore, a sore gum that had

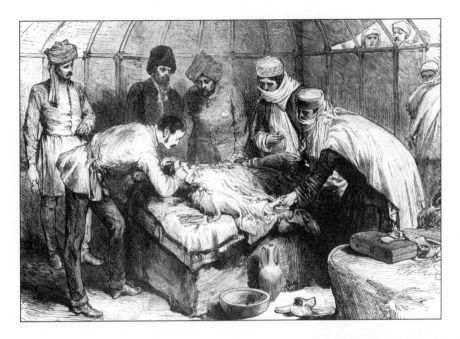

A patient sedated with chloroform undergoes an operation. Anesthesia allowed pain-free surgery.

been bothering him stopped hurting. In writing up the results of this experiment, Davy suggested that nitrous oxide "may probably be used with advantage during surgical operations."[55]

No one paid attention to this idea. Word of nitrous oxide's enjoyable effects spread, however, and some young people in Britain and the United States began to hold what were called laughing gas frolics. Sometimes people at these drug parties breathed a gas called ether instead of nitrous oxide. Both substances also became part of the shows put on by traveling medicine sellers. The showmen gave the gases to volunteers, who then made fools of themselves onstage as audiences watched.

"THIS IS NO HUMBUG"

The first person to use one of these gases to deaden pain during surgery was probably

British chemist Humphry Davy (1778–1829) found that nitrous oxide was an effective painkiller.

Crawford Long, a country doctor in Georgia. In 1842 he let a young man named James Venable breathe ether before he removed a tumor from his neck. Long then gave ether to patients before several other operations. He did not describe his procedure until 1849, however. By then, others had discovered the benefits of anesthesia.

Horace Wells, a dentist in Hartford, Connecticut, first saw nitrous oxide at work in 1844 in a traveling medicine show. Wells's acquaintance had volunteered to inhale the gas; while he was onstage during the show, he fell and cut his leg badly. He told Wells afterward that he had not noticed the injury until the effects of the gas wore off. Intrigued, Wells had the show's owner give him nitrous oxide and then had a tooth pulled from his mouth. He felt no pain during the extraction. "A new era of tooth pulling!"[56] Wells cried joyfully.

Wells persuaded a Boston surgeon, John Warren, to let him demonstrate the effects of nitrous oxide on a dental patient. Warren gave Wells his chance in front of a group of medical students at Massachusetts General Hospital in early 1845. Unfortunately, the patient did not receive enough gas, and he cried out when the tooth extraction began. The students drove Wells from the room with shouts and laughter.

The man who finally succeeded in bringing anesthesia to the world's surgeons was another dentist, William Morton. Morton, a friend of Wells, worked with ether rather than nitrous oxide. He tested it on himself, one of his patients, and his dog. He, too, then talked Warren

Nineteenth-century American dentist Horace Wells was the first to use nitrous oxide as an anesthetic in dentistry.

into letting him do a demonstration, although both Warren and his students understandably had their doubts after Wells's failure. On October 16, 1846, Morton successfully used ether to put a patient to sleep while Warren removed a tumor from the man's neck. At the end of the operation, the awestruck surgeon proclaimed, "Gentlemen, this is no humbug [fake]."[57] Word of the new technique spread quickly to Europe, and surgeons there as well as in the United States were eager to use it. American physician/writer Oliver Wendell Holmes gave the invention the name *anesthesia*. The word means "lack of feeling" in Greek.

NEW ANESTHETICS

Shortly after Morton's succcessful demonstration, James Simpson, a Scottish obstetrician, discovered that a third substance, chloroform, was also a good anesthetic. Like ether, chloroform was breathed as a gas made when liquid placed on a face mask evaporated. Simpson found that chloroform smelled better and was less irritating to the patient than ether. He urged that it be given to women going through the painful process of childbirth.

Some religious leaders objected to using anesthesia during childbirth, saying the Bible demanded that women suffer while giving birth. However, after Britain's Queen Victoria agreed to be anesthetized during the birth of her seventh child in 1853 and spoke highly of the experience, childbirth anesthesia became popular.

Anesthesia was a godsend during major surgery. It could be dangerous for patients, however, and rendering people unconscious for minor operations seemed an unnecessary risk. Researchers therefore looked for drugs that could be used to numb only part of the body. In 1884 an Austrian eye specialist named Carl Koller found that a compound named cocaine could do this job during eye surgery. Cocaine was made from a South American plant called coca, so the doctor's discovery earned him the nickname "Coca Koller." More effective local anesthetics, as such drugs came to be called, were developed later.

SURGERY UNLIMITED

British surgeon John Erichsen claimed in 1873 that "the abdomen, the chest and the brain [will] be for ever shut from the intrusion of the wise and humane surgeon"[58] because the risk of infection and other complications following such surgery was still so high. By the end of the century, however, improvements in asepsis and surgical techniques meant that these areas were no longer off-limits. During the late nineteenth century, surgeons such as the German Theodor Billroth and the American William Halsted developed many operations that surgeons continued to perform into the twenty-first century. Medical historian Roy Porter writes that, freed from the twin barriers of pain and infection, "surgery changed more in the nineteenth century than in the previous two thousand years."[59]

Nineteenth-century scientists' journeys into the body gave doctors a better understanding of health and disease than had ever been possible before. Physicians were beginning to work from facts rather than guesses. Nonetheless, except for some surgical operations and other treatments such as antiserums, doctors remained better at preventing and identifying diseases than at curing them. Cures had to wait for the century to come.

Chapter

6 The Age of Specialization

By the last decades of the nineteenth century, medicine was growing so quickly and in so many arenas that no one person could keep track of it all. As a result, more and more doctors began to specialize. Some chose certain parts of the body or certain classes of patients, such as women or children. Others focused on certain diseases or particular medical conditions, such as childbirth. Researchers, too, specialized more than ever before. As a result, late-nineteenth- and early-twentieth-century medical practice was a colorful patchwork of advances in many fields. A number of these specialities were new, created by advances in medicine.

MYSTERY RAYS

One new specialty, radiology, was begun by a German professor who had no interest in medicine at all. His name was Wilhelm Röntgen, and he taught physics at the University of Würzburg. In 1895 he was studying cathode rays, the glowing radiation given off by a device called a Crookes tube. A Crookes tube is a sealed glass tube from which most of the air has been removed, creating a vacuum inside.

The cathode rays appeared when an electric current was passed through the tube.

Röntgen wanted to find out whether a Crookes tube produced any kind of radiation (energy) besides cathode rays. On the afternoon of November 8, he put black paper around the tube to block out the cathode rays' distracting light. He also darkened his laboratory. He then turned on the electricity that ran through the tube.

To his surprise, Röntgen saw a screen coated with a fluorescent material, lying a yard or two away from the Crookes tube, start to glow with a dim green light. The tube, he decided, must be giving off invisible rays that passed through the paper and affected the screen. Cathode rays had never been known to do this at such a distance.

Feverishly Röntgen began experimenting with the mystery radiation. He knew that cathode rays could darken or expose photographic film, in effect making a photograph. He therefore tried letting the new rays fall on a sheet of film. He found that they, too, exposed it, leaving an outline of objects placed between the rays and the film. During the next few weeks he learned that the rays could pass through most materials that blocked light and still expose the film. Only lead seemed to stop these

German physicist Wilhelm Röntgen's discovery of X rays in 1895 allowed doctors to see inside their patients' bodies without surgery.

ence journal on December 28. A week later, the story was making headlines throughout the Western world. One newspaper called his discovery "a marvellous triumph of science."[61]

A HELP AND A DANGER

Physicians realized the importance of Röntgen's discovery at once. Here was a way to see inside the living body, something that had never been possible before without surgery. Within months, doctors began using X rays to examine broken bones and search for foreign objects such as bullets in the body. H. J. W. Dam, a writer for *McClure's Magazine* in the United States, claimed that X rays were "a greater blessing to humanity than even the Listerian antiseptic system of surgery."[62] Röntgen received the first Nobel Prize in physics in 1901 for his discovery.

During the next several decades, researchers built and improved machines that took medical photos with X rays. Inventors, meanwhile, found ways to make the rays show some of the body's soft tissues as well as bones. A picture of the digestive system could be made, for example, after a patient swallowed compounds of barium, another element that proved able to block the rays. X-ray photos, taken in hospitals and some doctors' offices, became a vital tool in diagnosis. Specialists who made and interpreted them came to be called radiologists.

Physicians also began using Röntgen's mystery rays for the treatment of certain conditions. Röntgen had reported that

rays. Most amazing of all, when he placed his wife's hand on the film and let the rays pass through, the resulting photo clearly showed the bones inside. A fainter outline marked the flesh of her hand. Otto Glasser, a biographer of Röntgen, wrote, "She could hardly believe that this bony hand was her own and shuddered at the thought that she was seeing her skeleton. To Mrs. Röntgen, as to many others later, this experience gave a vague premonition of death."[60]

Röntgen did not know what his new rays were, and X in science stands for something unknown. For this reason, he decided to call the radiation *X rays*. He published a description of them in a sci-

MEDICAL USES OF X RAYS

As this excerpt from a German newspaper shows, physicians and surgeons realized at once how useful X rays could be to them. The translated article is quoted in W. Robert Nitske's The Life of Wilhelm Conrad Röntgen.

"The surgeon . . . could determine the extent of a complicated bone fracture without the manual [by hand] examination which is so painful to the patient. He could find the position of a foreign body, such as a bullet or a piece of [gun] shell, much more easily than had been possible heretofore and without any painful examinations with a probe. Such [X ray] photographs also would be extremely valuable in diagnosing bone diseases . . . and would help to guide the way in therapy [treatment]."

exposure to high doses of the rays burned the skin, so some doctors used X rays to remove unwanted skin growths. The successful use of X rays led some physicians to try other types of radiation as well. For example, radium, discovered in 1898 by French physicists Marie and Pierre Curie, also came to be used in medicine because of the radiation it gave off. Researchers found in 1904 that radiation killed cancer cells faster than it killed normal ones, so radium and, later, other radioactive materials were applied to cancer treatment.

Unfortunately, as growing numbers of radiologists and some of their patients found out, X rays and other types of radiation could be dangerous. High doses produced sores on the skin that would not heal. Sometimes the radiation caused so much damage that people died. Marie Curie was among those slowly poisoned by her discovery.

Furthermore, repeated exposure to even low doses of radiation could produce can-

Marie Curie (pictured), along with her husband Pierre Curie, discovered the radioactive element radium in 1898.

cer many years later. Some people described the danger of high-dose radiation soon after X rays came into use, but the threat from low doses was not recognized until the 1920s. By then, many people had been unknowingly sickened because X rays, for instance, had been used for such trivial purposes as removing unwanted body hair.

DEADLY MOSQUITOES

While some specialists focused on treating diseases, others worked at preventing them. One specialty that was particularly important in this area was tropical medicine. This field developed around the end of the nineteenth century, chiefly because governments of Western nations wanted to protect the health of settlers in the colonies that the countries were establishing in Africa, Asia, and other tropical regions of the world.

Tropical medicine benefitted colonists and native peoples alike. Moreover, because some "tropical" diseases affected health in the colonists' home countries, the work of specialists in this field reached far beyond the tropics. Malaria and cholera, for instance, had caused many deaths in Europe; yellow fever, which probably came to the New World aboard slaves ships from Africa, produced regular epidemics in the southeastern United States.

In the course of investigating these diseases, tropical medicine specialists discovered one of the final pieces in the puzzle of how epidemics were caused and spread. In

British doctor Ronald Ross investigated the theory that malaria was spread by a microscopic parasite.

1877 Patrick Manson, a British physician working in China, had shown that elephantiasis, a disfiguring disease caused by a tiny parasite, was spread by mosquitoes when they bit people and sucked their blood. This was the first time a disease was proved to be transmitted by an insect.

Manson suggested to Ronald Ross, another British doctor who worked in India, that malaria might be spread in the same way. A French army surgeon named Charles Laveran had already demonstrated in 1880 that malaria was caused not by "bad air" as its name indicated but by a microscopic parasite. Testing Manson's idea, Ross examined hundreds of mosquitoes under a microscope. Finally, on August 20, 1897, he found the parasite's eggs in the stomach of one. He termed this time of triumph "Mosquito Day" and penned a short rhyme in celebration:

> I know this little thing
> A myriad [very many] men will save
> O Death, where is thy sting?
> Thy Victory, O Grave?[63]

Ross worked with a form of malaria that affected birds, but about a year later, two Italians, Giovanni Grassi and Amico Bignami, proved that the parasites that caused malaria in humans also spent part of their lives in a certain species of mosquito. These two researchers worked out the parasites' complex life cycle and showed exactly how the disease was transmitted. With the mosquito's role in transmitting malaria proven, the way to prevent infections became clear: Reduce the number of mosquitoes in an area. The easiest way to do this was to remove or poison pools of stagnant water, where mosquito larvae developed.

A bust sculpture of Walter Reed of the American army, the surgeon and bacteriologist who determined how yellow fever was spread.

SAVING THE PANAMA CANAL

In 1881, even before the riddle of malaria had been solved, a Cuban doctor named Carlos Finlay had suggested that yellow fever, which was common in Cuba, was spread by mosquitoes. But not until 1898, when the United States occupied Cuba after winning the Spanish-American War, did anyone prove Finlay's theory. Out of concern for the health of its soldiers, the U.S. army ordered a group of researchers headed by physician Walter Reed to try to find out how the disease was spread. Army officials hoped that if its method of transmission could be discovered, the deadly sickness could be controlled.

Reed's group performed experiments that tested Finlay's mosquito theory as well as a competing belief that yellow fever was spread through materials soiled by sick people. Because no animal had been known to catch yellow fever, the researchers used human volunteers, who allowed themselves to be bitten by mosquitoes that had fed on people who had the disease. The experiments proved that mosquitoes, although a different type from the ones that spread malaria, did transmit yellow fever.

The Reed commission's work led to a mosquito-killing campaign that controlled the disease in Havana, the Cuban capital, in less than a year. Just a few years later the same techniques served the United States equally well elsewhere. In 1904 the United States took over the building of the Panama Canal from the French, who had abandoned the project in 1888, partly because so many of their workers were dying from malaria and yellow fever. The antimosquito program

MOSQUITO DAY

In this excerpt from the Cambridge Illustrated History of Medicine, *edited by Roy Porter, British physician Ronald Ross describes the first time he saw the microscopic parasites that cause malaria in the stomach of a mosquito. Ross's discovery, which proved that mosquitoes could transmit this serious disease, took place on August 20, 1897, which he always remembered as "Mosquito Day."*

"At about 1 p.m. I determined to sacrifice . . . Mosquito 38, although my eyesight was already fatigued. . . .

The dissection was excellent, and I went carefully through the tissues, now so familiar to me, searching . . . with the same passion and care as one would search some vast ruined palace for a little hidden treasure. Nothing. . . . But the stomach tissues still remained to be examined . . . a great white expanse of cells like a great courtyard of flagstones, each of which must be scrutinized [examined carefully]—half an hour's labour at least. I was tired, and what was the use? I must have examined the stomachs of a thousand mosquitoes by this time. But the Angel of Fate fortunately laid his hand on my head; and I had scarcely commenced the search again when I saw a clear and almost perfectly circular outline before me. . . . The outline was much too sharp, the cell too small to be an ordinary stomach-cell of a mosquito. I looked a little further. Here was another, and another exactly similar cell. . . . *In each of these cells there was a cluster of small granules, black as jet* [a semiprecious black stone] and exactly like the black pigment granules of the *Plasmodium* crescents [the parasites known to cause malaria]. . . . I counted twelve of the cells, all of the same size and appearance and all containing exactly the same granules. Then I made rough drawings of nine of the cells . . . , scribbled my notes, sealed my specimen, went home to tea . . . , and slept solidly for an hour. . . .

When I awoke with mind refreshed my first thought was: Eureka! the problem is solved!"

implemented by American health officials wiped out yellow fever in the area by 1906. Building of the canal resumed, and this vital waterway opened in 1913.

THE PUZZLE OF THE CHICKENS

Other specialties affected the lives of Europeans and Americans to an even greater extent than tropical medicine did. One was nutrition, which concerned the foods people ate and the way these foods affected the body. Many nineteenth-century scientists believed that the human diet needed to contain only proteins, fats, carbohydrates, and certain mineral salts. When Paris was besieged during a civil uprising in 1871, however, a physician named J. B. H. Dumas learned the hard way that this was not enough. Unable to find milk for a nursery full of hungry babies, he tried to feed them on a solution of fat, sugar (carbohydrate), and egg white (protein). In spite of his efforts, the children died. Clearly something was missing from this minimal but supposedly complete diet.

Evidence of what that "something" was began to mount around the start of the twentieth century. An illness called beriberi, common among poor people in Asia, provided a clue. The arms and legs of people with beriberi felt weak and numb. Their bodies swelled, and finally their hearts failed.

Christiaan Eijkman, a doctor working in the Dutch colony of Batavia, on the south Asian island of Java, was studying beriberi in the 1890s. At the time, scientists thought a microbe caused the disease. Eijkman, however, noticed that some chickens in the yard of a local hospital were becoming weak and falling down, much as people with beriberi did.

HOPEFUL START FOR A CENTURY

On New Year's Eve, 1900, Walter Reed wrote a letter to his wife, Emilia, describing his excitement at having shown how the epidemic disease yellow fever was spread. Charles-Edward Amory Winslow quotes Reed's letter in The Conquest of Epidemic Disease.

"Only ten minutes more of the old century remain. Here have I been sitting [in Cuba], reading that most wonderful book, *La Roche on Yellow Fever*, written in 1853. Forty-seven years later it has been permitted to me and my assistants to lift the impenetrable veil that has surrounded the causation of this most wonderful [astonishing], dreadful pest of humanity and to put it on a rational and scientific basis. I thank God that this has been accomplished during the latter days of the old century. May its cure be wrought out in the early days of the new."

Patients in a yellow fever hospital in Havana, Cuba, around 1899. Soon after this photo was taken, a mosquito extermination program curbed the disease in Havana.

These chickens, he learned, had been fed rice that was "polished," or freed from its natural husks, because their regular food had run out. Normally they would have received brown or "rough" rice, which still had its husks.

Eijkman returned the chickens to their diet of rough rice and found that their symptoms disappeared. Following up on his guess that beriberi was connected to diet, Eijkman next wrote to the managers of all the prisons on Java, asking them what they fed their prisoners and whether they had many cases of beriberi. He learned that beriberi was common in 71 percent of prisons using polished rice. However, only 3 percent of those in prisons that used unpolished rice had the disease. What unpolished rice actually contained that prevented beriberi remained a mystery, however.

"Vital Amines"

Eventually, in 1912, Polish-born biochemist Casimir Funk purified the substance in rice husks that prevented or cured beriberi. He believed that lack of this chemical or similar ones caused not only beriberi but several other mysterious diseases such as scurvy, which had been common among sailors on long sea voyages.

Funk was not the first person to link scurvy with diet. A British navy surgeon named James Lind had suggested in the eighteenth century that this disease was caused by the sailors' limited diet. He wrote in 1753,

> [An] extremely powerful cause, observed at sea to occasion [produce] this disease, . . . is, the want [lack] of fresh vegetables and greens. . . . Experience indeed sufficiently shews [shows], that

Eighteenth-century British navy surgeon James Lind, standing, gives citrus fruit to sailors with scurvy.

as greens or fresh vegetables, with ripe fruits, are the best remedies for [scurvy], so they prove the most effectual preservatives [means of prevention] against it.[64]

Since green vegetables could not be stored on ships, Lind advised giving sailors lemons or limes to cure or prevent scurvy. (In time, British sailors became known as "limeys" because of this seemingly odd part of their ships' rations.)

Funk thought that compounds like the one he had found in rice husks belonged to a group of chemicals called amines. He therefore called them *vitamines*, short for "vital amines." Later, when chemists learned that some of these substances were not amines, the word was changed to *vitamins*. Though Funk may have been wrong about the amines, the "vital" part of his idea was certainly correct.

A number of vitamins were identified during the first half of the twentieth century. Scientists were also able to figure out which diseases were caused by the absence of which vitamins. For instance, they found that scurvy occurred when vitamin C (ascorbic acid) was missing from the diet. An absence of vitamin B_1 (thiamin) produced beriberi.

It now became clear that many of the health problems of poor people were caused by malnutrition. These problems could be prevented or cured by providing certain foods or, starting in the 1930s, pure vitamins in pill form. Vitamin deficiency diseases are now rare in industrialized countries except among the poorest groups. However, they remain a problem in parts of the world where food is scarce.

CHAINED LIKE ANIMALS

Most of the developing specialties focused on the physical health of people. But a new medical specialty, psychiatry, focusing on mental health also had major effects on society. Psychiatrists are physicians who study and treat mental illness, or disorders of the mind.

Traditionally, families or charities had taken care of most mentally ill people. Those with no one to care for them were often chained like wild animals in grim institutions such as London's Bethlehem Hospital, nicknamed Bedlam. Beginning in the late eighteenth century, however, reformers such as Philippe Pinel in France and, later, Dorothea Dix in the United States worked to free the mentally ill from their chains. They advised placing these patients under the care of gentle but strong-minded supervisors who would teach them how to behave in society. By no means all mental patients received this improved treatment, however, and even those who did were seldom cured of their illness.

Although observations and experiments were revealing the causes of physical disease, the causes of mental illness remained mysterious. By the nineteenth century, most people no longer believed, as many in previous centuries had, that "madness" or "insanity" came from being possessed by demons or cursed by angry gods. Instead, some experts thought mental illness was caused by unhealthy habits of thought or behavior. Others believed mental illness was inborn in certain families.

The idea that mental illness was a medical condition (or group of conditions), probably due to brain damage, developed slowly during the nineteenth century. The medical specialty of psychiatry appeared toward the century's end. Psychiatrists such as Emil Kraepelin in Germany gave scientific descriptions of various forms of mental illness. These included mania, marked by excitement and wild activity, and melancholy or depression, marked by feelings of sadness and despair. No one knew, however, whether these illnesses had the same cause or different ones.

TALKING CURES

Near the end of the nineteenth century, some psychiatrists began to explore the idea that some types of mental illness resulted from events or thoughts in a person's past rather than from physical damage to the brain. The most important of these thinkers was an Austrian named Sigmund Freud. Freud dealt mostly with the relatively mild type of mental illness called neurosis.

Beginning in the late 1890s, Freud claimed that neurosis was caused by sexual thoughts that occurred in early childhood. Because these thoughts did not seem morally acceptable, he said, people put them out of their awareness. Freud believed, however, that the thoughts remained buried in a part of the mind that he termed the unconscious. From there, they distorted conscious thought, producing neurosis. Bringing these hidden thoughts and memories back into consciousness would cure the illness, Freud maintained. He developed a technique called free association, in which people responded to a spoken word by saying the first other word that occurred to them, as a way of recovering these memories. He also unearthed memories by analyzing patients' dreams, which he called the "royal road to the unconscious."[65]

Freud's treatment regimen, which he called psychoanalysis, was widely publicized and hotly discussed in both Europe and the United States. Psychoanalysis did far more than offer a new way to treat mental illness, however. Because Freud

---

KINDER TREATMENT FOR MENTAL ILLNESS

Philippe Pinel, a physician who treated the mentally ill in Paris in the early nineteenth century, protested the cruel treatment these patients often received. In this excerpt from his Treatise on Insanity *(1801), translated by D. D. Davis in 1806 and reprinted in Logan Clendening's* Source Book of Medical History, *Pinel describes what he thinks is a better approach.*

"Public asylums for maniacs [institutions caring for the mentally ill] have been regarded as places of confinement for such of its members as are become dangerous to the peace of society. The managers of those institutions, who are frequently men of little knowledge and less humanity, . . . have been permitted to exercise towards their innocent prisoners a most arbitrary system of cruelty and violence; while experience affords ample and daily proofs of the happier effects of a mild, conciliating treatment, rendered effective by steady and dispassionate [calm] firmness. . . .

The accomplishment of this scheme would be most effectually obtained by combining with every lunatic asylum, the advantage of an extensive enclosure, to be converted into a sort of farm, which might be cultivated at the expence of the patients, and the profits of which might be devoted to their support. A principal hospital of Spain, presents in this respect an excellent example for our imitation. The maniacs, capable of working, are distributed every morning into separate parties [groups]. An overlooker is appointed for each class, who apportions [assigns] to them all, individually, their respective employments, directs their exertions, and watches over their conduct. The whole day is thus occupied in salutary [healthful] and refreshing exercises, which are interrupted only by short intervals of rest and relaxation. The fatigues of the day prepare the labourers for sleep and repose during the night. Hence it happens, that those whose condition [social status] does not place them above the necessity of submission to toil and labour, are almost always cured; whilst the grandee [nobleman], who would think himself degraded by any exercises of this description, is generally incurable."

Austrian psychiatrist Sigmund Freud pioneered a technique known as psychoanalysis for treating patients with neuroses.

claimed that everyone, not just the mentally ill, had childhood sexual thoughts to some degree, his ideas challenged and changed the way people thought about themselves. Some were shocked by his stress on sex, which they felt that "nice" people should not think about. Others were startled to hear that past thoughts,

seemingly completely forgotten, could affect present thinking and behavior.

Some psychiatrists trained by Freud helped to spread his ideas. Others such as Alfred Adler and Carl Jung broke with him and proposed ideas of their own. All treated mental illness primarily through repeated conversations between the psychiatrist and the patient. Treatment could last for years.

These "talking cures,"[66] as one early patient called them, became popular among well-educated people, especially in the United States. They sometimes seemed to help people with mild mental illness, but they did little for those whose problems were more severe. Some people called them unscientific because the ideas on which they were based could not be proved. Psychiatrists of the early twentieth century had little else to offer, however. "We know a lot and can do little,"[67] one said in 1910.

All these new specialties, and many others, broke important new ground in understanding the body and mind. Some led to better knowledge and treatment of disease. They paved the way for the even greater achievements of the mid–twentieth century, the time when medicine made what were probably its greatest advances in history so far.

Chapter

7 Midcentury Triumphs

Until well into the 1930s physicians could prevent some diseases but cure very few. Physician-writer Lewis Thomas, a medical student in the 1930s, wrote that at that time,

> Our task for the future [as physicians] was to [give] diagnoses and explanation. Explanations were the real business of medicine. What the ill patient

and his family wanted most was to know the name of the illness, and then, if possible, what had caused it, and finally, most important of all, how it was likely to turn out.[68]

Doing something to change how the course of an illness turned out usually was not part of the picture.

Then, ironically, just as people were fighting World War II, the most destructive war the world had yet known, medicine began to make great strides. Suddenly medical science seemed poised to conquer many of humanity's worst killers. People saw doctors almost as gods. Many believed that, in the near future, medicine would let people live nearly forever.

MAGIC BULLETS

The greatest triumphs came in treating those old enemies, infectious diseases. For the first time, specific diseases were being cured. Paul Ehrlich, a German researcher, had developed the first modern medicine to attack a specific disease in the early 1900s. Ehrlich wanted to replace the toxic and fairly ineffective drugs then used to treat the sexually transmitted disease

German bacteriologist Paul Ehrlich (left) developed the drug Salvarsan to treat syphilis.

Dr. Gerhard Domagk (left) won a Nobel Prize in 1939 for his discovery of the antibacterial effects of Prontonsil.

syphilis. He and his coworkers made and tested hundreds of compounds. Finally—on his 606th try, in 1907—he found one that worked. He later gave his "Compound 606" the name of Salvarsan. By 1910, some ten thousand people had been treated with it. Salvarsan was not completely effective or safe, but it was much better than the earlier drugs. Also an expert on the immune system, Ehrlich compared Salvarsan to substances in immune serum that acted as what he called "magic bullets"[69] to destroy particular bacteria. After Salvarsan's success, many researchers hoped to find "magic" drug "bullets" that would affect other microbes.

Even greater advances followed. For example, in 1932 Gerhard Domagk, a scientist working for a German dye and chemical company, found that a red dye called Prontonsil cured mice injected with streptococci, a common kind of bacteria

that causes wound infections and other ailments. When Domagk's daughter suffered an infection with these same microbes, Domagk healed her as well.

Domagk described his experiments with Prontonsil in a scientific paper in 1935. Other researchers then analyzed the substance. They found that the dye contained a compound called sulfanilamide and that this was what affected microbes. This substance did not kill bacteria, but it kept them from multiplying. That gave the body's immune system time to destroy the existing organisms. Scientists soon developed several related compounds that did the same for the kinds of bacteria that sulfanilamide did not affect. This group of drugs, which became known as the sulfa drugs, halted a number of life-threatening infections. These drugs may well have changed the course of history, since one saved the life of British prime

Scottish bacteriologist Alexander Fleming discovered the antibiotic penicillin in 1928.

minister Winston Churchill when he fell ill during World War II.

A SPECK OF MOLD

While the sulfa drugs were being hailed as miracle workers, a description of an even more powerful "magic bullet" lay forgotten in medical archives. In August 1928 Alexander Fleming, a Scottish bacteriologist, had returned to his London laboratory after a vacation to find that one of his cultures of bacteria appeared to be ruined. A bluish speck of a common mold called *Penicillium*, often found on stale bread, had somehow landed on the culture dish and started to grow there. Colonies of bacteria still made most of the dish's surface look cloudy. Around the patch of mold, however, there was a clear ring where no bacteria grew. In fact, when Fleming looked at the culture under a microscope, he could see that the bacteria in this area were dying. He wrote later,

When I saw those bacteria fading away, I had no suspicion that I had got a clue to the most powerful therapeutic [healing] substance yet used to defeat bacterial infections in the human body. The appearance of the culture was such, though, that I knew it should not be neglected.[70]

Fleming realized that the mold must be making something that killed the bacteria. He tried to purify the substance, which he called penicillin. He finally produced a tiny amount, but the process was difficult. Worse still, penicillin appeared to lose its bacteria-killing power when combined with blood. It therefore seemed unlikely to succeed as a drug. Fleming wrote an article about his find for a scientific journal in 1929, then turned to other, unrelated work.

About ten years later, just as World War II was starting in Europe, two researchers at Britain's Oxford University were studying a phenomenon called antibiosis, the process in which the bodies of some living things make substances that kill others. The scientists, an Australian named Howard Florey and a Jew who had recently escaped from Nazi Germany, Ernst Chain, hoped that their work might uncover drugs that could fight infection in wounded soldiers.

While searching the medical literature for examples of antibiosis, Florey and Chain unearthed Fleming's report. At first they found making penicillin just as hard as Fleming had, but they did not give up. They tested the drug in mice in 1940 and found that, contrary to its failure in Fleming's test tubes, it killed bacteria very effectively in living bodies.

Norman Heatley, another member of Florey and Chain's research group, discovered better methods to extract penicillin from mold. Using a jury-rigged collection of milk churns, lemonade bottles, bedpans, and a bathtub, the group began trying to make enough penicillin to treat a human being. They first tested the drug on a policeman who was dying of a wound infection. After four days the man seemed well on his way to recovery.

American researchers began to mass-produce penicillin in 1941. Here, a scientist shelves incubated bottles of Penicillium notatum, *the mold from which penicillin is derived.*

Unfortunately, the supply of penicillin then ran out. The infection returned, and the patient died. Later tests in five other people, however, produced three cures. Florey called the results "almost miraculous."[71]

Florey tried to interest British drug manufacturers in mass-producing penicillin. They were doing other war work, though, and did not want to risk resources on a new product. So in July 1941 Florey took his idea to the United States. Heatley worked with American government researchers and drug companies to create ways to produce penicillin in larger amounts. Tests showed that this drug destroyed a wide range of bacteria. For instance, it reduced the death rate from bacterial pneumonia from 30 percent to 6 percent.

During World War II the limited supply of penicillin was given mostly to wounded soldiers. After the war, however, the drug was made available to everyone. By then other similar drugs, now called antibiotics, were also appearing. One of these was streptomycin, made by a mold living in soil. Selman Waksman, a Russian-born scientist working in the United States, discovered it in 1944. Streptomycin proved able to kill microbes not affected by penicillin, including one of humankind's most stubborn foes, the bacteria that cause tuberculosis. Thanks to antibiotics, the war against bacterial diseases seemed sure to end in victory.

The Tiniest Killers

Victory was less clear in the case of diseases caused by recently discovered microorganisms called viruses. During most of the nineteenth century, the word *virus* had meant any kind of disease-causing poison produced by a living thing. After 1884, however, the term was used to refer to a still-unidentified class of organisms. Scientists knew that viruses were extremely small, since they would pass through a filter that could hold back bacteria. Researchers concluded that viruses caused a number of human diseases. For instance, James Carroll, a member of Walter Reed's yellow fever commission, showed in 1901 that that disease was caused by a virus. Influenza, which caused a terrible pandemic in 1918 that within six months killed three times as many people as had died in World War I, was also a viral disease.

Even though scientists knew viruses existed, they could not see them until the 1930s, when the electron microscope, which can magnify objects by as much as a million times, was invented. Scientists also found ways to grow cultures of viruses during this decade. They learned that, unlike bacteria, viruses can reproduce only inside living cells.

Antibiotics did not affect viruses, and the search for other drugs that would do so proved frustrating. Once again, preventing infection proved to be the answer, through the use of vaccines.

Some vaccines, such as those against smallpox and rabies, had been around for a long time. Others, such as one against yellow fever, were developed in the early twentieth century. One important killer virus remained at large, however: the one that caused infantile paralysis, or poliomyelitis—"polio" for short. Beginning

A MIRACLE CURE

In this excerpt from
The Health Century,
*Edward Shorter
describes one of the
first successful uses of
the antibiotic drug
penicillin in the
United States. Part of
the description is
quoted from* Pfizer:
An Informal
History *by Samuel
Mines.*

"By 1943 word of penicillin is getting out. People know it can save dying relatives and call desperately for it. Yet the government has reserved the [small] supply for research on civilians and for military needs. What, therefore, was Pfizer [an American drug company that had just started making penicillin] executive John Smith supposed to do when Dr. Leo Loewe, a physician at the Brooklyn Jewish Hospital, came to him and pleaded for penicillin to 'save the life of a doctor's small daughter' dying of an infection of the valves of the heart? . . . Smith said he'd come and see the little girl. His heart melted [and he gave Loewe the penicillin].

'For three days Dr. Loewe administered penicillin to the dying child . . . , dripping it into a vein from a hanging bottle twenty-four hours a day. Her condition improved.' They continued giving her enormous amounts. 'During those days, as the color came back to her face, Smith . . . came, day after day, to watch a miracle—the first human being to be snatched from death's sure grip by his company's own penicillin.'"

around the start of the twentieth century, polio epidemics appeared almost every summer, especially in the United States. As many as fifty thousand children were infected each year in that country alone. Many died or were paralyzed for life.

In 1950 an American charity organization, the National Foundation for Infantile Paralysis, launched a research project to develop a vaccine against the disease. In fact, two vaccines were created as a result of this project. Jonas Salk of the University of Pittsburgh, "a slight [small] man who radiated a sort of restless eagerness and energy,"[72] according to a man who knew

him, developed the first, an injectable vaccine, made from killed polio viruses. Russian-born Albert Sabin of the University of Cincinnati, meanwhile, invented a second vaccine that used living viruses that were weakened (attenuated) so that they could not cause disease.

Salk tried his vaccine on a small group, including his own children. "When you inoculate children with a polio vaccine, you don't sleep well for two or three months,"[73] he told reporters. That test went well, however, so Salk's research group proceeded with a much larger one, this time involving almost 2 million

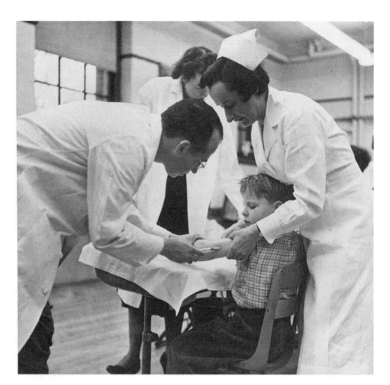

Jonas Salk (right) injects a child with his polio vaccine. Albert Sabin (below) developed an oral vaccine that provided permanent immunity to polio.

children. When success in the larger test was announced on April 12, 1955, church bells rang and factory sirens blared throughout the country.

Sabin's vaccine also was tested successfully. It proved even more effective, since unlike the Salk vaccine, Sabin's gave permanent immunity to the disease. Sabin's vaccine was also easier to administer, since it could be swallowed rather than having to be injected. Mass vaccination programs using one or both vaccines soon almost eliminated polio from the United States and other Western countries. The last naturally occurring case of polio in the United States was identified in 1979.

Drugs and vaccines were not the only midcentury success stories. Surgery, too, made great strides. Some of its advances were due to a discovery made near the century's start but not fully used until around World War II.

Brave physicians in earlier centuries had occasionally tried to transfuse, or transfer, blood from one person (or sometimes an animal) to another, but the patients usually died. In 1900 an Austrian doctor named Karl Landsteiner found out why. He noticed that, when blood from two people was mixed on a microscope slide, the oxygen-carrying red cells in the blood sometimes—but not always—formed clumps. In a living body, such clumping would have caused death.

By the time of Landsteiner's observation, researchers studying the immune system had learned that chemicals in the blood called antibodies attach themselves to other chemicals, termed antigens, located on the surface of microorganisms or other invaders. Each antibody attaches to only one type of antigen, marking the invader for destruction by the blood's white cells. Landsteiner found that red cells could carry two possible antigens, which he termed A and B. Some people's cells had only A, others had only B, and still others had neither. Later he also discovered that a

JUNIOR SCIENTISTS

When Leona Baumgartner, New York City's commissioner of health, interviewed children taking part in a controlled test of Jonas Salk's polio vaccine, she found that these "Polio Pioneers" understood the design of the test better than many adults. Baumgartner's account appears in Patenting the Sun, a book by Jane S. Smith that describes the development of the vaccine.

"I went down early because I was interested to see what the kids knew about this. . . . I walked into a classroom . . . and I said, 'What's going on here, anyway?' They were so excited about it, and they told me about it. They told me that part of the kids were going to get the real stuff [vaccine], and some part of them weren't going to get the real stuff, and nobody was going to know who got what. And all of the information would go out to Ann Arbor [the research headquarters], and out there they would know which stuff they got.

So I said, 'Gee, that sounds kind of dumb to me. Why do they give you stuff that isn't any good?' They were shocked, they had to correct me. And those youngsters [gave] as good a description of a controlled experiment as I've ever heard. I was very excited, because it seemed to me that if you could teach a generation of kids about what a controlled experiment was, and about what science really was, this was a plus value regardless of whether the vaccine was any good or not."

few people's cells carried both antigens. If people received blood containing an antigen different from their own, an immune reaction occurred, producing the clumping he had seen.

Landsteiner quickly realized that his finding could be used to predict whether a blood transfusion would succeed. A technician merely had to mix samples of the donor's and receiver's blood on a slide and see whether clumping occurred. If it did not, the transfusion would probably work. Landsteiner showed that people from what he called blood group A (that is, those whose red cells carried only the A antigen) could not exchange blood with people in blood group B. Transfusions from people whose cells carried neither antigen, which he called blood group O (for zero), could safely be given to anyone. These people could receive blood only from other people in group O, however. People whose cells carried both antigens—group AB—on the other hand, could receive blood from anyone but could give it only to other members of their own group.

Landsteiner's discovery made blood transfusions possible. For decades they were seldom used, however, because blood could not be preserved for any length of time. Finally, in the 1930s, improved preservation methods made it possible to store, or bank, blood for relatively long periods. The first blood bank was created in 1937.

At about the same time, researchers found ways to extract and preserve plasma, another name for the liquid part of blood. This discovery was especially important during World War II because plasma, unlike whole blood, could be given to people of any blood type. It also could be taken onto a battlefield as a powder, then made into ready-to-use liquid just by adding sterile water. Plasma could prevent or reverse a condition called shock, which often killed people after they had lost blood from severe wounds. During shock, the circulatory system collapses because it does not contain enough fluid. Plasma restored the needed liquid. According to one wartime report, soldiers near death from shock could receive plasma and "would be sitting up and talking, with all the life and color back in their faces"[74] a few minutes later. Both

Austrian pathologist Karl Landsteiner won the 1930 Nobel Prize for his discovery of the human blood-group system.

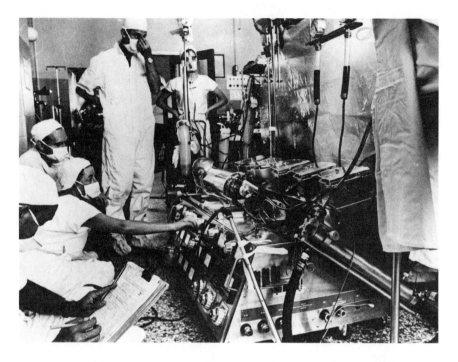

Medical workers keep watch over the heart-lung machine during a heart operation in 1968. The heart-lung machine was invented by John Gibbon and first used in 1953.

plasma and blood transfusions greatly reduced deaths from blood loss among soldiers with battle wounds.

STOPPING THE HEART

Blood and plasma transfusions also greatly reduced deaths during and after surgical operations. Surgery on most parts of the body had become routine by midcentury, but there was one major exception: the heart. Surgeons could sometimes sew up stab wounds in the heart (the first to do so was an African American surgeon, Daniel Williams, in 1893), but lengthy operations could not be done on a beating heart. The heart could not be stopped during surgery, either, because its pumping action was needed to keep blood and its life-giving oxygen moving through the body. The brain could be permanently damaged by just four minutes without oxygen.

These problems ruled out most heart surgery until a Philadelphia surgeon named John Gibbon invented a machine that temporarily took over the work of the heart and lungs. The vein that normally led into the heart was attached instead to the machine. Now, instead of being pumped to the lungs by the heart, blood went through the machine, which added oxygen and removed carbon dioxide, just as the lungs would normally do. The machine then pumped the blood back into the body through the aorta, the body's chief artery. Thanks to Gibbon's machine, the heart could be stopped safely during even a long operation.

On May 6, 1953, Gibbon used his heart-lung machine while he sewed up a hole (a birth defect) in the heart of eighteen-year-old Cecilia Bavolek. She recovered completely. After that well-publicized triumph, open heart surgery advanced quickly. Surgeons first used the machine while they repaired heart valves that had been damaged by disease. In the 1960s they became able to bypass and replace parts of the coronary arteries that had been blocked by fatty deposits, a major cause of heart attacks.

MEDICINE'S DARK SIDE

The change in medicine's power between the 1940s and the 1960s was greater than any that had ever happened before. The advances dazzled the public, and even many doctors, into forgetting that the profession still had many unfinished tasks. There was still little that could be done, for instance, for most people with heart disease or cancer, which had become the industrialized world's greatest killers. Moreover, the medical miracles that saved lives in wealthy countries still had not reached the rest of the world.

Medicine's triumphs also made people forget that medical science could have a dark side. It had its share of accidents, as when a batch of an early polio vaccine containing full-strength virus gave the disease to about eighty children. Worse still, some physicians intentionally took part in terribly unethical acts. In Germany and Japan during World War II, for example, doctors did painful experiments on prisoners of war and concentration camp inmates. In a notorious experiment in the United States, doctors secretly withheld antibiotics from hundreds of African Americans with syphilis from the 1930s to the 1970s in order to study the progress of the disease. When these scandals were revealed, rules about human testing were revised. They now state that people in such tests must always be told the risks they run and must always consent to taking those risks.

Still, people in the Western world could hardly be blamed for their midcentury excitement over medical progress. Lewis Thomas wrote that when he first became a physician in the 1930s,

> The major threats to human life were tuberculosis, tetanus, syphilis, rheumatic fever [an infection that often caused joint and heart problems], pneumonia, meningitis, polio, and septicemia [blood poisoning, or bodywide infection] of all sorts. These things worried us the way cancer, heart disease and stroke worry us today. The big problems of the 1930s and 1940s have literally vanished.[75]

Medical science was the reason why.

Chapter

8 Changes and Challenges

Medicine moved in many directions during the last decades of the twentieth century. Some of its "midcentury miracles" became almost routine. Others have proved to work less well than people had at first hoped. New fields such as gene therapy now hold the promise of medical advances greater than any that have come before. At the same time, many old problems remain unsolved, and new challenges such as AIDS have joined them.

WORLDWIDE CAMPAIGNS

Once infectious diseases were reduced in the West, some organizations tried to repeat that success on a global scale. These attempts produced one great victory. In 1966 the World Health Organization (WHO), a part of the United Nations, set the ambitious goal of eradicating, or wiping out, smallpox worldwide. WHO volunteers spent thirteen years working their way through rain forests and deserts, flooded rivers and city slums around the world. They tracked down every outbreak of the disease and vaccinated people in the area to stop it from spreading. In 1977 WHO announced its success. This was the first time a disease had been completely destroyed by deliberate human action. "It showed that we could eradicate a disease in . . . poor countr[ies] in spite of inadequate health services," said Nick Ward, a leading member of the WHO team. "Provided one can mobilize the . . . creative energy of a people, . . . anything is possible."[76] A similar program aimed at vaccinating the world's children against polio, measles, diphtheria, tetanus, whooping cough, and tuberculosis has also met with some success. WHO hopes to eradicate polio by 2005.

Other worldwide disease-fighting efforts have not worked as well. In the hopeful days of midcentury, many people thought malaria and other diseases carried by insects could be controlled by killing the carriers with powerful new insecticides such as DDT (dichloro-diphenyl-trichloroethane). WHO, in fact, began a campaign to wipe out malaria in 1957. For a while, the program seemed to be succeeding. Mosquitoes, however, soon developed resistance to the chemicals, which also proved harmful to the environment. Similarly, the malaria parasites developed resistance to modern forms of quinine (the drug first made

CHANGES AND CHALLENGES ■ 95

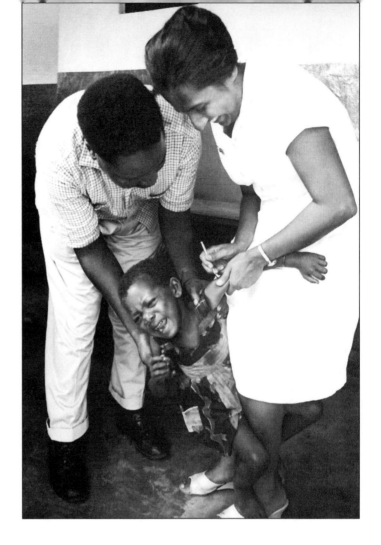

A young boy is vaccinated against smallpox in Dar es Salaam, Tanzania, in 1965.

from cinchona bark) that had killed them before. The number of malaria cases worldwide began rising once more in the late 1960s, and in the 1990s there were three times as many cases of malaria as there had been in 1961, the height of the malaria program's success. Today, malaria affects almost 40 percent of the world's people. It causes almost 3 million deaths a year and saps the strength of those it does not kill. The disease affects the poor disproportionately. "It is malaria that keeps Africa down,"[77] one doctor said in 1997.

A DEADLY PANDEMIC

Even in industrialized countries, it has become clear that U.S. surgeon general William Stewart's claim in 1967 that the United States could soon "close the book on epidemic diseases"[78] was far from correct. The greatest new challenge from the world of microbes is acquired immune deficiency syndrome, or AIDS. This disease first came to medical attention in 1981, when doctors in San Francisco reported seeing unusual infections in young homosexual men. Similar illnesses soon appeared in other groups, including people who regularly injected drugs and people who had recently had blood transfusions. These were all diseases that a normal immune system could fight off. It seemed likely, therefore, that some underlying illness had destroyed the people's immune systems.

Scientists suspected that a virus caused this seemingly new disease, and teams of researchers raced to isolate it. In early 1984, French scientist Luc Montagnier and his coworkers identified what became known as human immunodeficiency virus, or HIV. Most doctors believe that this virus causes AIDS. Researchers have shown that it is spread through contact with blood or sexual fluids.

Montagnier's group and a research team led by Robert Gallo in the United States quickly developed a test that could identify HIV in blood. Using this test, blood bank managers could detect virus-contaminated blood and remove it from the supply used for transfusions. Doctors could also identify people who had been infected with HIV but did not yet show

WIPING OUT SMALLPOX IN AFGHANISTAN

In Quest for the Killers, *June Goodfield quotes Donald Henderson, the leader of the World Health Organization (WHO) project to eradicate smallpox, as he recalls the courage of WHO vaccination team members in one of the project's most difficult countries.*

"When it came down to saying where would be the last case [of smallpox] in the world, I was confident it would be Afghanistan. But two men and two women disproved my prediction. An Indian ex-colonel and a Pathan [Afghani] physician organized the program [in Afghanistan] superbly, sending teams of vaccinators systematically through the countryside until they had made three complete circuits of Afghanistan. They even got to women in purdah [seclusion required by the Muslim religion] by a mixture of carrot and stick, but no force was ever used. Had it been, they would have been shot. The two women—a Burmese nurse, four and a half feet tall, and a six-foot Russian—worked in the most remote areas and in impossible situations. The Russian was stoned [stones were thrown at her] and barely escaped with her life; the Burmese would travel on horseback with a gun over her shoulder—for decoration only—which was both longer and taller than she. But they were brilliant. . . . Such was the ingenuity of these four that smallpox was eradicated in Afghanistan two years before Asia [as a whole] was cleared."

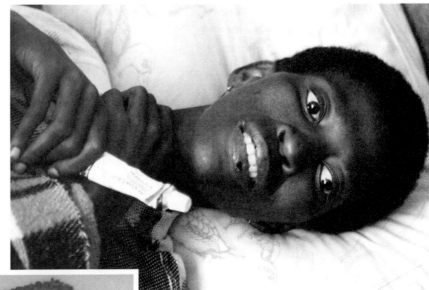

(Below) A microscopic view of the human immunodeficiency virus (HIV). (Right) This South African female AIDS patient is one of the millions living with HIV in sub-Saharan Africa.

fectious diseases today. Health education and screening of banked blood have reduced the number of new cases in most industrialized countries. However, social disruption, war, and other problems have turned AIDS into a pandemic in Africa and Asia. About 70 percent of the 36.1 million men, women, and children estimated to be living with HIV infection in 2000 were in sub-Saharan Africa. The effect of the pandemic alarms many. "AIDS is reversing decades of progress [in] improving the quality of life in developing countries,"[79] Martha Ainsworth, a senior economist of the World Bank, said in 1997.

Attempts to make a vaccine for AIDS have failed so far because HIV mutates constantly, changing its antigens in the process. "Cocktails" combining several drugs can sometimes control the disease and extend life, but the drugs are very expensive and have many side effects. The virus has also become resistant to many

signs of AIDS. This was important because HIV can stay in a person's body for years before destroying enough immune cells to cause illness. Thus, a person with HIV can spread the virus while still seeming to be healthy.

AIDS is perhaps the most serious and certainly the best known threat among in-new drugs almost as fast as they have been developed.

MICROBES STRIKE BACK

Some researchers fear that AIDS is just the first of a new wave of infectious diseases. Several "new" viral diseases, including the dramatically deadly Ebola fever, have made media headlines in the last several decades. So far, none has stricken large numbers of people the way AIDS has, but that luck could change. Rising populations, war and civil strife, and growing industrialization are pushing people into places where humans have seldom gone. Their activities are changing these environments greatly. As a result, people may encounter deadly microbes that are new to them. Jet travel could then spread these germs around the world in days.

Furthermore, old microbial foes that had seemed to be defeated are rising to battle medicine once again. Common bacteria, such as those that cause wound infections and tuberculosis, have become resistant to the antibiotics that once controlled them. This development of resistance is a natural part of the evolutionary war between humans and microbes. For instance, an antibiotic may kill most microbes of a certain type. However, a few of these germs will, by chance, have some feature, such as a difference in their chemistry, that allows them to survive. These microbes will reproduce, while the nonresistant ones fail to do so. As a result, the number of resistant germs will grow over time. Scientists are frantically searching for new types of antibiotics, but so far they have had limited success.

In spite of these fears, medicine in industrialized countries during the late twentieth century turned away from the infectious diseases that had preoccupied it for most of its history. Its focus changed to long-term, or chronic, illnesses such as heart disease and cancer. These diseases, which most often affect old people, have become the leading causes of death in such countries because growing numbers of people live long enough to develop them. Doctors have had much less luck in treating these illnesses than they have had with infectious diseases.

One field in which doctors have had success, however, has been organ transplantation. Thanks to this new form of surgery, organs destroyed by disease can be replaced with healthy ones. The organs usually come from people who died suddenly, most often in accidents, and left permission for the organs to be removed.

Although organ transplants are a modern success story, the idea of such operations is hardly new. French surgeon Alexis Carrel and American physiologist Charles Guthrie transplanted hearts and other organs experimentally in animals in the second decade of the twentieth century. They worked out ways to perform the tricky task of connecting the transplanted organs to the nerves and blood vessels of their receivers. Surgeons built on these techniques to reattach parts of people's own bodies that had been cut off by accident. Transplants from one person to another seemed almost impossible, however, because the immune system destroys anything that it sees as not part of a person's body. By mid-century, immunologists (scientists who study the immune system) felt that the only transplant likely to stay healthy would be one from a person's identical twin. Identical twins have exactly the same genes, so they are indistinguishable as far as the immune system is concerned. The first successful organ transplant in humans did in fact involve identical twins. A kidney transplant between twin brothers took place in 1954.

Most people, of course, do not have an identical twin. Scientists therefore looked for ways to rein in the immune system so that it would not destroy a transplanted organ from an unrelated person. The first method that did not destroy the immune

French surgeon Alexis Carrel's experiments with organ transplant in animals paved the way for human transplants.

system almost completely was a drug called azathioprine. Along with hormones that suppressed the immune system, this drug was used in the first successful kidney transplant between unrelated people, which took place in 1962. Transplants of livers and lungs followed.

TRANSPLANTING THE HEART

The most exciting transplant of all was the heart. Hearts are the hardest organs to transplant because they start to break down within minutes after death. Other organs, by contrast, can be preserved on ice for several hours. The first heart transplant took place on December 3, 1967, in Cape Town, South Africa. There, surgeon Christiaan Barnard removed the heart from a young woman whose brain had been destroyed in a traffic accident and placed it inside Louis Washkansky, a dying fifty-three-year-old man who had suffered three heart attacks. Barnard wrote later,

> My moment of truth—the moment when the enormity of it all really hit me—was just after I had taken out Washkansky's heart. I looked down and saw this empty space. . . . The realization that there was a man lying in front of me without a heart but still alive was, I think, the most awe-inspiring moment of all.[80]

Unfortunately, Washkansky lived only eighteen days before dying of a lung infection that his weakened immune system could not fight off. His transplanted heart had not been rejected at the time of his

The first human heart transplant was performed by Dr. Christiaan Barnard on December 3, 1967.

death, however. His surgery created a worldwide sensation (*Newsweek* called it the "miracle in Capetown"[81]) and inspired a host of similar operations.

Dramatic as they were, transplants, especially heart transplants, had limited success in the 1970s. Transplant surgery became fairly common only in the 1980s, after a new immune-suppressing drug called cyclosporine, which came from a mold that a researcher found in a piece of dirt, was developed. This drug kept the immune system from rejecting transplants, yet left some of its strength free to fight infections. Liver transplant pioneer Thomas Starzl called cyclosporine "the key that unlocks the door to transplants."[82]

Organ transplantation is still difficult. People who receive transplants must take cyclosporine or similar drugs all their lives. These drugs are costly and have side effects, chiefly limiting the power to resist infection. Sometimes the transplants are rejected in spite of the drugs. Worst of all, there are far fewer organ donors than there are people who need transplants. Would-be transplant patients must often wait months or years, and some die before an organ can be found for them. When transplants succeed, however, they can restore dying people to almost normal lives.

INHERITED INFORMATION

A new kind of treatment called gene therapy may, in future years, dwarf even the excitement that surrounded antibiotics and transplants. Gene therapy means treating disease by changing genes, the units of inherited information inside each cell that determine the traits or characteristics of a living thing. A living thing's genome, or complete collection of genes, is like a blueprint for that particular organism. The first step in gene therapy is being able to "read" the relevant parts of that blueprint, but only in the latter half of the twentieth century did that become possible.

People have always known that members of families often look alike and have other features in common. The scientific study of the way traits are inherited, however, began only in the middle of the nineteenth century, when a monk named Gregor Mendel bred pea plants in the garden of his monastery in Brno (now part of the Czech Republic). Mendel studied how height, for instance, varied in the offspring

Nineteenth-century Austrian monk and botanist Gregor Mendel bred pea plants to show how traits are passed from parent to offspring.

of a tall plant mated with a short plant. After studying many generations of peas, he worked out simple rules to describe how inherited "factors" were passed from parent plants to their offspring.

Mendel published his rules in 1865, but almost no one read his work. It attracted much more notice when several other scientists, also studying patterns of inherited traits, rediscovered his studies in 1900. During the next two decades, researchers in the United States showed that genes were carried in wormlike bodies called chromosomes, which are found in the nucleus of each body cell. A unit of heredi-

tary material that determines one trait came to be known as a gene. The new scientific specialty that studied inheritance of traits was called genetics.

THE CODE OF LIFE

By the mid-1940s, scientists had determined that genes were made up of a complex molecule, deoxyribonucleic acid (DNA). The structure of DNA remained a mystery, however. Scientists needed to solve this mystery in order to find out how genetic information was coded and reproduced in DNA. The first to do so were two men at Britain's prestigious Cambridge University, a young American named James Watson and a somewhat older Briton named Francis Crick. They found that a DNA molecule is shaped like a twisted ladder. The sides are made up of a chemical called phosphate, and the steps are pairs of smaller molecules called bases. This overall shape is often called the "double helix." Remembering the day he and Crick made their groundbreaking discovery, Watson wrote,

> Upon his arrival [in their office] Francis did not get more than halfway through the door before I let loose that the answer to everything was in our hands. . . . We both knew that we would not be home [sure that their proposed structure was right] until a complete model was built. . . . The implications . . . were too important to risk crying wolf. Thus I felt slightly queasy when at lunch Francis winged

into the Eagle [a local bar] to tell everyone . . . that we had found the secret of life.[83]

Watson and Crick published a paper describing the structure of DNA in the British science journal *Nature* on April 25, 1953. Five weeks later they proposed that a DNA molecule reproduces itself by splitting down its length, like a zipper opening. Each half then attracts chemicals in the nucleus to build a new half. This idea was later shown to be correct. DNA's power to reproduce lets a cell duplicate its genome when it divides into two new cells.

Scientists also found out how DNA encodes inherited information. There are four bases in DNA: adenine, cytosine, guanine,

LIVING WITH A NEW HEART

Lael Wertenbaker, in To Mend the Heart, *describes the special courage and energy with which one early heart transplant patient, forty-five-year-old Richard Cope, met the challenges of recovering from his surgery in 1970 and the treatments he had to undergo to keep his body from rejecting his new heart. Part of her description is quoted from an article about Cope in a 1974 issue of* Medical World News.

"Cope's recovery was remarkable. He was soon up, 'bounding around,' and within three weeks was hiking, as measured by a pedometer, fifteen miles a day within the hospital. Less than five weeks after his transplant he booked a plane ticket home. . . .

He played golf. Once he flipped over in a snowmobile. ('I thought everyone was going to have a heart attack!') He traveled whenever he pleased by air and took only one special precaution. 'I make sure I have my pills in my hand! They may lose your luggage. They lost mine once with my medication in it. The guy said to me, "We'll have it for you in a couple of days." I said, "Don't bother. I'll be dead in a couple of days." So they put on a special flight to run my luggage up.'. . .

Cope lived through rejection episodes. . . . He shrank from five foot eight to five five as vertebrae collapsed in his back from prednisone [a hormone]-induced calcium depletion. The essential prednisone, while suppressing the rejection function, softened his bones to allow 'backbone compression' and he suffered from cracked and broken ribs. Nevertheless, four years after his transplantation, Cope said, 'I wake up, and it's teeming [pouring] rain and I hold my face up to it. Hey, what a lousy day? Lousy? Man, if I open my eyes to that day, it's a great day!'"

and thymine. Adenine always pairs with thymine, and cytosine always pairs with guanine. In 1957 Crick suggested that information is coded in the order, or sequence, of bases within each DNA molecule. Each group of three bases is a "letter" in the code. "Such an arrangement can carry an enormous amount of information,"[84] he said. The cell uses this coded information as a guide when making the many different proteins that do the work of the cell. A gene came to be defined as a group of bases—usually about a thousand—that holds the code for one protein. Later studies showed that some genes have jobs other than making proteins, such as controlling the action of other genes.

CHANGING GENES

At first the study of genes had little direct effect on medicine. In the early 1970s, however, scientists found out how to change genes as well as study them. Working first with bacteria, the scientists transferred genes from one cell to another, even when the cells belonged to different types of living things. By adding human genes to bacteria, this genetic engineering, as it was called, turned the microbes into factories that made compounds that some people's bodies lacked, such as human insulin. Some of these substances had been very expensive because they had to be taken from slaughtered animals, and each animal yielded only a tiny amount. Others came from donated blood, which could be contaminated. Genetic engineering gave people who needed these substances a cheaper, safer source for them.

Even more important, genetic engineering meant that doctors might be able to change genes within the human body. Scientists had learned that some illnesses are caused by defective genes inherited from

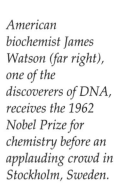

American biochemist James Watson (far right), one of the discoverers of DNA, receives the 1962 Nobel Prize for chemistry before an applauding crowd in Stockholm, Sweden.

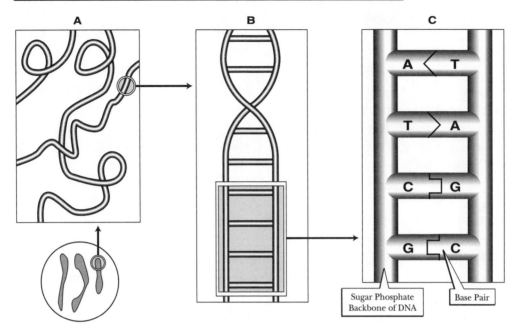

Rungs on a Ladder: The Structure of DNA

A.

B.

C.

Sugar Phosphate
Backbone of DNA

Base Pair

A. A chromosome is a chainlike strand of DNA, which contains many genes.

B. When the chromosome is greatly magnified under a microscope, it looks like a long ladder that is twisted into a double helix. The twisting allows these amazingly long strands to fit inside a single tiny cell.

C. The sides of the DNA ladder are made of sugar and phosphate molecules. Between the two sides are rungs made up of the four base pairs—AT, TA, GC, and CG. The letters stand for the four bases that make up the pairs: adenine, guanine, cytosine, and thymine. A single strand of DNA may contain billions of rungs. The different arrangements of these four base pairs are codes that call for different combinations of amino acids. Amino acids combine to make up proteins, which, in turn, shape the endless variety of features that make up every living thing. Each sequence of base pairs that contains the instructions for making a single protein is called a gene.

one or both parents. If some of these genes could be replaced with normal ones, people with those diseases might be helped. The idea of gene therapy was born.

The first successful human gene therapy took place on September 14, 1990. The patient, a four-year-old girl named Ashanthi deSilva, had no immune system because a defective gene kept her body from making a protein that the immune system must have. Children with this condition catch one infection after another, and they usually die at an early age.

W. French Anderson and other researchers from the National Institutes of Health, the U.S. government's chief research institution, took blood from Ashanthi. In their laboratory they put healthy genes with the code for the missing protein into her white blood cells. Then, while she watched *Sesame Street* on a hospital TV, they sent the cells back into her blood. The treatment did not completely cure her, but it greatly improved her health. With the help of follow-up treatments, French Anderson wrote in 1995, Ashanthi was "transformed from a quarantined little girl, who was always sick and left the house only to visit her doctor, into a healthy, vibrant nine-year-old who loves life and does *everything*."[85] Ashanthi was still reported to be healthy in the late 1990s.

Most attempts at gene therapy since then have not been as successful. Such treatments seem to help people with some inherited diseases, however, such as cystic fibrosis. Many doctors think gene therapy will become an important way to treat other illnesses, such as cancer and AIDS, as the twenty-first century advances.

LINKING PAST AND FUTURE

Gene therapy, organ transplants, and other high-technology treatments offer exciting hopes for the future. Medical historian Roy Porter writes, "At the cutting edge—bio-technology, genetic engineering and so forth—medicine is the moving frontier, not simply of science and healing but of the future of mankind."[86] High-tech medicine also presents problems, however. Some critics say it encourages doctors to see patients as machines or examples of disease rather than as people. High-tech treatments also are very expensive. Some physicians feel that the money they cost should be spent on preventing disease rather than trying to cure it. Funds could be used to help mothers bear and raise healthy babies, for instance, or could finance programs that teach habits such as eating more fruits and vegetables and avoiding smoking.

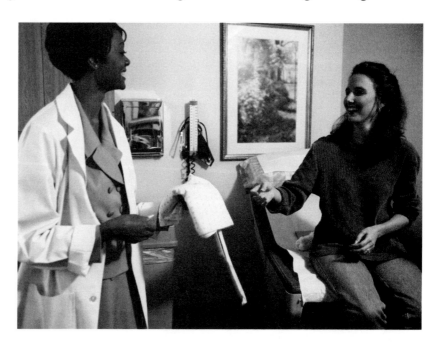

Some doctors feel that medicine should focus on preventative care rather than expensive treatments.

A FATHER'S FEARS

In Correcting the Code, *a book about the early years of gene therapy, Larry Thompson describes the feelings of Raj deSilva, the father of the four-year-old girl who was to receive one of the world's first attempts at such therapy, on the night before the treatment took place in September 1990.*

"Exhausted from travel and anticipation, Raj and Van [Raj's wife] barely spoke to each other about what would happen in the morning. As they settled into the Children's Inn for the night, neither wanted the other to know how nervous he or she had become. . . .

Raj lay in bed that night running everything through his head. He still hated that Ashi [his daughter] would be the first to try this revolutionary experiment. Yet, the risks seemed small and the promise great. If gene therapy worked, one day she could stop taking the painful, weekly PEG-ADA shots [which supplied the chemical her body lacked] that, at $4,000 an injection, threatened to consume her lifetime health insurance maximum, leaving her uninsured forever. And there was the hope that one day, because of gene therapy, she would lead a normal life. 'But at the back of your mind, you worry: "Is it going to turn out right?" Nobody's done this before. It is not a proven treatment. There are risks involved. But you say, "Well I have thought this thing out. I have talked to the doctors. I have a good feeling about them. It's going to be OK."'

Eventually, he fell asleep."

High-tech or not, medicine today has learned much from its past. The best doctors still study patients as carefully as Hippocrates did. Many give people the same suggestions for maintaining health that physicians of ancient Greece, India, and China did, though the reasons they offer may be different. Researchers still use the scientific method developed by Aristotle and the thinkers of the Renaissance and Enlightenment. Scientists and physicians alike depend on technology and procedures invented in the nineteenth century, from microscopes and X rays to antisepsis and anesthesia. They explain disease by talking about germs, cells, and genes. And doctors save lives daily by using twentieth-century advances such as antibiotics and organ transplants. Medicine is sure to build on all this knowledge still further as it faces the many challenges of the centuries to come.

Notes

Chapter 1: The Dawn of Medicine

1. Quoted in Roberto Margotta, *The History of Medicine*. New York: Smithmark, 1996, p. 12.

2. Quoted in Roy Porter, *The Greatest Benefit to Mankind: A Medical History of Humanity*. New York: Norton, 1997, p. 151.

3. Quoted in Albert S. Lyons and R. Joseph Petrucelli, *Medicine: An Illustrated History*. New York: Abrams, 1987, p. 121.

4. Quoted in Porter, *The Greatest Benefit to Mankind*, p. 155.

5. Quoted in Lyons and Petrucelli, *Medicine*, p. 216.

6. Quoted in Porter, *The Greatest Benefit to Mankind*, p. 62.

7. Quoted in Lyons and Petrucelli, *Medicine*, p. 213.

8. Quoted in Porter, *The Greatest Benefit to Mankind*, p. 70.

9. Quoted in Porter, *The Greatest Benefit to Mankind*, p. 77.

Chapter 2: Rebirth

10. Quoted in Porter, *The Greatest Benefit to Mankind*, p. 88.

11. Quoted in Porter, *The Greatest Benefit to Mankind*, p. 111.

12. Quoted in Lyons and Petrucelli, *Medicine*, p. 310.

13. Quoted in Porter, *The Greatest Benefit to Mankind*, p. 124.

14. Quoted in Andrew Nikiforuk, *The Fourth Horseman: A Short History of Epidemics, Plagues, and Other Scourges*. London: Phoenix, 1993, p. 56.

15. Quoted in Porter, *The Greatest Benefit to Mankind*, p. 171.

16. Quoted in Porter, *The Greatest Benefit to Mankind*, p. 202.

17. Quoted in Margotta, *The History of Medicine*, p. 82.

18. Quoted in Porter, *The Greatest Benefit to Mankind*, p. 181.

19. Quoted in Lyons and Petrucelli, *Medicine*, p. 213.

20. Quoted in Margotta, *The History of Medicine*, p. 91.

21. Quoted in Porter, *The Greatest Benefit to Mankind*, p. 244.

Chapter 3: Medicine Becomes a Science

22. William Harvey, *An Anatomical Essay on the Motion of the Heart and Blood in Animals*. Trans. Robert Willis, rev. Alexander Bowie. In the Harvard Classics, *Scientific Papers*, vol. 38. New York: Collier, 1910, p. 129.

23. Harvey, *An Anatomical Essay*, p. 106.

24. Quoted in Margotta, *The History of Medicine*, p. 108.

25. Quoted in Porter, *The Greatest Benefit to Mankind*, p. 224.

26. Samuel Hoole, trans., *The Select Works of Antony van Leeuwenhoek*, vol. 1. New York: Arno Press, 1977, p. 118.

27. Quoted in Frederic Lawrence Holmes, *Lavoisier and the Chemistry of Life*. Madison: University of Wisconsin Press, 1985, p. 193.

28. Quoted in Porter, *The Greatest Benefit to Mankind*, p. 266.

29. Quoted in Logan Clendening, ed., *Source Book of Medical History*. Mineola, NY: Dover, 1960, p. 421.

30. Quoted in Porter, *The Greatest Benefit to Mankind*, p. 229.

31. Quoted in Porter, *The Greatest Benefit to Mankind*, p. 293.

Chapter 4: Invisible Enemies

32. Quoted in Porter, *The Greatest Benefit to Mankind*, p. 399.

33. Quoted in Porter, *The Greatest Benefit to Mankind*, p. 401.

34. Quoted in Margotta, *The History of Medicine*, p. 157.

35. Quoted in Porter, *The Greatest Benefit to Mankind*, p. 411.

36. Quoted in Charles-Edward Amory Winslow, *The Conquest of Epidemic Disease: A Chapter in the History of Ideas*. Madison: University of Wisconsin Press, 1980, p. 273.

37. Quoted in Ralph R. Frerichs, John Snow website, UCLA, Dept. of Epidemiology, School of Public Health, www.ph.ucla.edu/ epi/snow. html.

38. Rob DeSalle, ed., *Epidemic! The World of Infectious Disease*. New York: New Press/American Museum of Natural History, 1999, p. 66.

39. Quoted in Jenny Sutcliffe and Nancy Duin, *A History of Medicine*. New York: Barnes & Noble, 1992, p. 62.

40. Quoted in Laurence Farmer, *Master Surgeon*. New York: Harper & Brothers, 1962, p. 46.

41. Quoted in Clendening, *Source Book of Medical History*, p. 621.

42. Quoted in Porter, *The Greatest Benefit to Mankind*, p. 597.

43. Quoted in René Vallery-Radot, *The Life of Louis Pasteur*. Trans. Mrs. R. L. Devonshire. Garden City, NY: Garden City Publishing, 1927.

44. Quoted in Margotta, *The History of Medicine*, p. 158.

45. Porter, *The Greatest Benefit to Mankind*, p. 428.

Chapter 5: Journeys into the Body

46. Quoted in Porter, *The Greatest Benefit to Mankind*, p. 331.

47. Quoted in Porter, *The Greatest Benefit to Mankind*, p. 340.

48. Quoted in Porter, *The Greatest Benefit to Mankind*, p. 343.

49. Quoted in Porter, The Greatest Benefit to Mankind, p. 341.

50. Quoted in Roy Porter, ed., *The Cambridge Illustrated History of Medicine*. Cambridge, England: Cambridge University Press, 1996, p. 174.

51. Quoted in Lyons and Petrucelli, *Medicine*, p. 521.

52. Quoted in Porter, *The Greatest Benefit to Mankind*, p. 311.

53. Quoted in Sutcliffe and Duin, *A History of Medicine*, p. 46.

54. Quoted in René Fülöp-Miller, *Triumph over Pain*. Trans. Eden and Cedar Paul. Indianapolis: Bobbs-Merrill, 1938, p. 168.

55. Quoted in Porter, *The Greatest Benefit to Mankind*, p. 366.

56. Quoted in Sutcliffe and Duin, *A History of Medicine*, p. 47.

57. Quoted in Sutcliffe and Duin, *A History of Medicine*, p. 47.

58. Quoted in Sutcliffe and Duin, *A History of Medicine*, p. 71.

59. Porter, *The Greatest Benefit to Mankind*, p. 360.

Chapter 6: The Age of Specialization

60. Quoted in Catherine Caufield, *Multiple Exposures*. London: Secker and Warburg, 1989, p. 4.

61. Quoted in Caufield, *Multiple Exposures*, p. 4.

62. Quoted in W. Robert Nitske, *The Life of Wilhelm Conrad Röntgen*. Tucson: University of Arizona Press, 1971, p. 128.

63. Quoted in Sutcliffe and Duin, *A History of Medicine*, p. 95.

64. Quoted in Clendening, *Source Book of Medical History*, p. 465.

65. Quoted in Sutcliffe and Duin, *A History of Medicine*, p. 119.

66. Quoted in Sutcliffe and Duin, *A History of Medicine*, p. 118.

67. Quoted in Porter, *The Greatest Benefit to Mankind*, p. 513.

Chapter 7: Midcentury Triumphs

68. Quoted in Porter, *The Greatest Benefit to Mankind*, p. 682.

69. Quoted in Porter, *The Greatest Benefit to Mankind*, p. 452.

70. Quoted in Donald Robinson, *The Miracle Finders*. New York: David McKay, 1976, p. 3.

71. Quoted in Meyer Friedman and Gerald W. Friedland, *Medicine's 10 Greatest Discoveries*. New Haven, CT: Yale University Press, 1998, p. 184.

72. Allen B. Weisse, *Medical Odysseys: The Different and Sometimes Unexpected Pathways to Twentieth-Century Medical Discoveries*. New Brunswick, NJ: Rutgers University Press, 1991, p. 172.

73. Quoted in Sutcliffe and Duin, *A History of Medicine*, p. 202.

74. Quoted in Douglas Starr, "Again and Again in World War II, Blood Made the Difference," *Smithsonian*, March 1995, p. 135.

75. Quoted in Porter, *The Greatest Benefit to Mankind*, p. 715.

Chapter 8: Changes and Challenges

76. Quoted in June Goodfield, *Quest for the Killers*. Boston: Birkhäuser, 1985, p. 241.

77. Quoted in Ellen Ruppel Shell, "Return of a Deadly Disease," *Atlantic*, August 1997, p. 49.

78. Quoted in Elizabeth Pennisi, "U.S. Beefs Up CDC's Capabilities," *Science*, June 7, 1996, p. 1,413.

79. Quoted in Associated Press, "AIDS Called Economic Threat in Third World," *San Francisco Chronicle*, November 28, 1997, p. A4.

80. Quoted in Peter Hawthorne, *The Transplanted Heart*. Chicago: Rand McNally, 1968, p. iii.

81. "The Heart: Miracle in Cape Town," *Newsweek*, December 18, 1967, p. 86.

82. Quoted in Melvin Berger, *The Artificial Heart*. New York: Franklin Watts, 1987, p. 31.

83. James D. Watson, *The Double Helix*. New York: New American Library, 1968, pp. 125–26.

84. Quoted in Victoria Sherrow, *Great Scientists*. New York: Facts On File, 1992, p. 135.

85. W. French Anderson, "Gene Therapy," *Scientific American*, September 1995, p. 124.

86. Porter, *The Greatest Benefit to Mankind*, p. 668.

Glossary

acupuncture: A traditional Chinese medical treatment in which needles are inserted at certain points in the body and manipulated to redirect the flow of the body's energy (*qi*).

AIDS (acquired immune deficiency syndrome): A disease caused by a virus (HIV) that destroys the immune system.

alchemy: An ancient combination of science and mysticism that was the forerunner of chemistry.

anatomy: The study of the structure of human or animal bodies.

anesthesia: Making a person unconscious or numbing a part of the body to stop pain.

anthrax: A disease caused by bacteria that chiefly affects cattle and other large farm animals but can also be fatal to humans.

antibiosis: The process in which the bodies of living things make substances that kill other living things.

antibiotic: A substance, usually coming originally from a microorganism, that destroys bacteria or stops their growth.

antibody: A substance made by the immune system that attacks microorganisms or other invaders.

antigen: A chemical on the surface of cells that triggers the formation of antibodies.

antisepsis: The technique of killing microorganisms to prevent infection.

antiserum: Serum from an animal that has been injected with a disease-causing microorganism; it protects others against that microorganism.

aorta: The human body's largest artery.

apothecary: Old name for a pharmacist or druggist.

artery: A blood vessel that carries blood away from the heart.

ascorbic acid: Vitamin C.

asepsis: The technique of keeping microorganisms out of the body in order to prevent infection.

autopsy: Dissection to determine the cause of death or the type of damage done by disease.

Ayurveda: The chief traditional medical system of India.

bacteria: A major group of microorganisms, some of which cause disease.

bacteriologist: A scientist who studies bacteria.

base: One of four types of small molecules that form part of DNA; the order of bases in the DNA molecule encodes inherited information.

beriberi: A disease caused by a lack of vitamin B_1 (thiamin) in the diet.

biochemistry: The study of chemical reactions in the bodies of living things.

Black Death: The epidemic of bubonic

and pneumonic plague that began in Europe in 1347.

blood bank: A place where blood and blood products are preserved and stored so that they will be available for transfusions.

blood group: One of a number of groups determined by the antigens on a person's red blood cells; the blood group affects whether the person can safely give or receive blood transfusions from others.

bubonic plague: An often-fatal disease caused by bacteria, marked by swellings and dark bruises on the body.

capillary: One of the microscopic blood vessels that connect arteries with veins.

carbohydrate: One of a group of compounds in food that contain carbon and hydrogen and help to provide energy for the body.

carbolic acid (phenol): A substance that can kill microorganisms on surfaces; it may also damage skin.

cathode rays: Rays given off by one electrode (the cathode) in a Crookes tube when an electric current is passed through the tube.

cell: The microscopic unit of which the bodies of all living things are made.

chloroform: An anesthetic substance widely used in the nineteenth century to ease the pain of childbirth.

cholera: A disease caused by bacteria that affects the digestive system and kills by draining the body of liquid; it is most often spread through drinking water.

chromosome: One of a number of worm-like bodies in the nucleus of a cell, containing inherited information in the form of DNA.

chronic disease: A disease that lasts a long time, often for the rest of a person's life.

cinchona bark (Jesuits' bark): The bark of a Peruvian tree, containing a substance (later named quinine) that kills the microscopic parasites that cause malaria.

circulation: Movement in a circle; often applied to the movement of blood in the body.

cocaine: A local anesthetic made from the coca plant, native to South America.

cold-blooded animal: An animal that is unable to control its internal body temperature and therefore is strongly affected by the temperature of its environment.

combustion: Burning; a process in which other matter is combined with oxygen.

compound fracture: A bone break in which part of the broken bone sticks out through the skin.

compound microscope: A microscope containing more than one lens.

contagious disease: A disease that is caused by microorganisms and can be spread by contact.

contract: To pull together and seemingly grow smaller, an ability that muscles have.

coronary artery: One of several arteries that provide blood to the heart.

cowpox: A mild disease that affects cows and, sometimes, humans; it is caused by a virus closely related to the one that causes smallpox.

Crookes tube: A sealed glass tube from which most of the air has been removed, creating a vacuum; it contains two electrodes, and an electric current can be passed through it.

culture: A laboratory colony of cells or microorganisms, often grown in a flat dish or in a test tube.

cyclosporine: A drug, originally made from a mold, that reduces the activity of the immune system; it is given to people receiving transplants to keep the immune system from destroying the transplanted organs.

cytoplasm: The jellylike substance inside the outer membrane, but outside the nucleus, of a cell.

DDT (dichloro-diphenyl-trichloroethane): A powerful insecticide that came into widespread use in the early 1940s; it was later found to be harmful to the environment and has been banned in some places.

depression: A mental illness marked by constant deep feelings of sadness and despair.

diagnose: To determine the cause of a disease or medical problem.

digitalis: A drug, originally made from the foxglove plant, that strengthens the heart and helps to remove the fluid that builds up in people whose hearts are failing.

diphtheria: A disease caused by a bacterium that killed many children until an antiserum was developed for it in the late nineteenth century.

dissection: Cutting apart a dead body, usually to learn about the structure and function of its parts.

DNA (deoxyribonucleic acid): The chemical that carries encoded inherited information in cells.

double helix: Two parallel coils, like a combination of a ladder and a corkscrew; the shape of a DNA molecule.

dropsy: Old name for swelling caused by a buildup of fluid in the body, which could be produced by heart failure, kidney failure, or other medical conditions.

Ebola fever: A deadly, but fortunately so far rare, virus-caused disease that produces bleeding throughout the body.

electron microscope: A microscope that uses a beam of electrons rather than light to form an image; it can magnify to a far greater degree than a microscope that uses light.

elephantiasis: A tropical disease caused by a tiny parasitic worm; the first disease proven to be transmitted by insects.

epidemic: The occurrence of a large number of cases of the same illness at about the same time.

eradicate: To destroy completely; make extinct.

ether: A chemical, usually in the form of a liquid that quickly evaporates into a gas, that produces insensitivity to pain and sometimes unconsciousness.

fermentation: A chemical process caused by microorganisms that breaks down complex substances from living things into simpler ones.

fertilized egg: The single cell from which a multicelled living thing develops, created when an egg cell and a sperm cell combine.

foxglove: A flowering plant from which the drug digitalis was originally made.

gastric juice: The acid liquid in the stomach that partly dissolves and breaks down food.

gene: The portion of a DNA molecule that carries the code for doing a single job, such as making one protein or controlling another gene.

gene therapy: Treating a disease by altering genes.

genetic engineering: The process of changing a genome by inserting or altering genes.

genetics: The study of inheritance of traits, including the processes and chemicals by means of which traits are passed on to offspring.

genome: A living thing's complete collection of genes.

germ: A microorganism.

germ theory of disease: The idea that some diseases are caused by microorganisms that invade and damage the body.

heart-lung machine: A machine that takes over the job of cleaning and adding oxygen to blood and pumping it through the body during surgery.

HIV (human immunodeficiency virus): The virus that most researchers believe is the cause of AIDS.

homeostasis: The power of the bodies of living things, especially of warm-blooded animals, to maintain a steady internal environment, thereby making themselves relatively independent of the outside environment.

humor: One of four body fluids that, according to the ancient Greeks, helped to control the health of the body; the humors were blood, phlegm, yellow bile, and black bile.

immune system: The body's defense system, made up of cells and chemicals in the blood and elsewhere.

immunologist: A scientist who studies the immune system.

infantile paralysis: An old name for poliomyelitis.

infection: Invasion by a disease-causing microorganism, or the disease caused by such an invasion.

infectious disease: A disease caused by a microorganism.

influenza: A disease caused by a virus that usually is not serious but has at times produced deadly epidemics.

Koch's postulates: A set of rules for finding out whether a certain microorganism causes a certain disease, first stated by German bacteriologist Robert Koch.

laughing gas: Nitrous oxide; so called because small doses of this gas make people feel happy and act foolish.

local anesthetic: A drug that makes part of the body unable to feel pain but does not make a person unconscious.

"magic bullet": A term created by German researcher Paul Ehrlich, referring to an immune system chemical or a drug that destroys a specific type of disease-causing microorganism.

malaria: A serious blood disease, caused by a microscopic parasite, that causes weakness, repeated attacks of fever, and sometimes death.

malnutrition: The condition resulting from having a diet that lacks vitamins or other substances needed for health.

mania: A mental illness marked by excitement and wild activity.

medicine: The profession of identifying, treating, and preventing disease.

melancholy: Another term for depression.

membrane: A thin layer of material that covers or surrounds something, such as a cell.

microbe: A microorganism.

microorganism: A living thing so small that it can be seen only with a microscope; most microorganisms consist of only a single cell.

midwife: A woman who helps other women give birth safely.

neurosis: A form of mental illness, usually fairly mild, that causes disturbing feelings such as anxiety.

nitrous oxide: A gas, sometimes called laughing gas, that produces happy feelings and insensitivity to pain in small doses and unconsciousness in larger doses; it was one of the earliest anesthetics.

nucleic acid: One of several chemicals that can encode inherited information.

nucleus: A central body in most cells, surrounded by a membrane and containing DNA and other chemicals.

nutrition: The study of the foods people eat and the ways that chemicals in food (or their absence) affect the body.

obstetrician: A physician who specializes in treating women in childbirth.

ophthalmoscope: A mirror device that allows a doctor to look inside a person's eye.

opium: A narcotic made from a type of poppy, used medically to relieve pain.

outbreak: A small epidemic.

pandemic: An epidemic that affects a large part of the world at about the same time.

parasite: A living thing that lives in or on another kind of living thing, taking its food from the other living thing and usually harming it.

pasteurization: A process of treating liquids with heat to kill microorganisms in them, invented by Louis Pasteur.

pathology: The study of the changes that disease makes in the body.

penicillin: An antibiotic drug, originally made from a type of mold, that destroys a wide range of disease-causing bacteria.

Penicillium: A group of molds or fungi, some of which make a substance that kills bacteria.

pharmacy: A business devoted to making medicines (drugs).

phosphate: A type of chemical that, among other things, forms the long sides or "backbones" of the DNA molecule.

physician: A person who practices the profession of medicine and, usually, has received special training to do so.

physiology: The study of the functions of the body.

plague: A deadly epidemic disease caused by bacteria; it can occur in bubonic, pneumonic, and other forms.

plasma: The liquid part of blood, after substances that make the blood clot have been removed.

pneumonia: A disease of the lungs that can be caused by a variety of microorganisms.

pneumonic plague: A form of plague that affects the lungs and can be spread through the air by coughs and sneezes.

poliomyelitis (polio): A disease caused by a virus that frequently causes death or paralysis (inability to move the muscles).

Prontonsil: A red dye discovered in the 1930s to stop the growth of certain bacteria; the active substance in it is sulfanilamide.

protein: One of a large group of chemicals that do various jobs in cells; proteins are also a necessary part of the human diet.

psychiatry: The medical specialty that treats mental illness.

psychoanalysis: A system of theories about and treatment for mental illness created by Sigmund Freud.

pulmonary artery: The vessel that carries blood from the heart to the lungs.

pulmonary vein: The vessel that carries blood from the lungs back to the heart.

pulse: A rhythmic beat, especially the heartbeat.

purge: A medical treatment that empties the bowels.

putrefaction: A process caused by microorganisms that decays or breaks down animal products such as dead bodies and meat.

qi (chi): According to traditional Chinese medicine, a form of energy that flows within the body along certain paths and affects the body's health.

quack: A person who falsely claims medical knowledge or the ability to treat disease.

quarantine: To separate living things from others in order to prevent the spread of disease.

quinine: A substance, originally made from cinchona bark, that kills the microscopic parasite that causes malaria.

rabies: A fatal brain disease caused by a virus and spread by the bite of infected animals.

radiation: Energy that certain atoms or molecules give off in the form of rays as they change internally; a number of types of radiation exist.

radioactivity: Radiation given off by certain atoms as they break down.

radiology: The medical specialty dealing with the study and use of X rays and other radiation.

radium: A radioactive element discovered by Pierre and Marie Curie in 1898.

red cell: A cell in the blood that carries oxygen through the body.

resistance: The power of a living thing to fight off or remain unaffected by something such as a drug; it usually can be passed on to offspring.

respiration: Breathing; also, the process by which oxygen is taken in and used by the body.

rickets: A bone disease caused by a deficiency of vitamin D.

Salvarsan: A drug to treat syphilis invented by Paul Ehrlich in 1907; it was the first modern drug that affected a specific kind of microorganism.

scientific method: The process of learning about nature by observing, forming explanations for what is observed, testing the explanations by further observation or experiment, and revising them as needed.

scurvy: A disease caused by a deficiency of vitamin C.

serum: The liquid part of blood.

shaman: An independent religious specialist who also often acts as a healer.

shock: An often-fatal medical condition caused by severe loss of blood or other body fluid, resulting in the collapse of the circulatory system.

smallpox: A serious epidemic disease caused by a virus that often produces death or permanent scarring.

spermatazoa: Male sex cells, or sperm.

stethoscope: A device that amplifies sounds in the chest.

streptomycin: An antibiotic, originally made from a mold, that kills a wide range of bacteria, including those that cause tuberculosis.

sulfa drugs: Sulfanilamide and related drugs.

sulfanilamide: A chemical that was found in the 1930s to stop the growth of several types of disease-causing bacteria.

syphilis: A serious, sexually transmitted disease caused by bacteria.

thiamin: Vitamin B_1.

tissues: Structures that are found in different parts of the body but have features such as texture in common; examples are blood and muscle tissue.

toxin: A poison, especially one made by living things such as microorganisms.

trachea (windpipe): The tube leading from the lungs to the throat.

trait: A characteristic of a living thing, usually inherited.

transfusion: The introduction of fluid, such as blood or plasma, into a blood vessel.

tropical medicine: The medical specialty dealing with diseases usually found in warm climates; some of these diseases also occur in milder climates.

tuberculosis: A serious disease, especially affecting the lungs, caused by a type of bacteria.

unconscious: The part of the mind that, according to Sigmund Freud, contains forgotten thoughts.

vaccination: The process of putting killed or weakened microorganisms into the body in order to help the immune system resist later attacks by that type of microorganism.

valve: An opening that can be changed to affect the flow of a liquid or that allows a liquid to flow in only one direction.

variolation: The process of introducing matter from smallpox (variola) sores into the body in the hope of causing a mild case of the disease and thereby preventing a serious one.

vein: A vessel that carries blood away from the heart.

ventricle: A lower chamber of the heart (humans have two).

virus: A very tiny microorganism, on the border between living and nonliving things, that can reproduce only inside living cells and sometimes causes disease.

vitamin: One of a group of chemicals that occurs in food and is necessary (in small amounts) for health.

vitamin B₁: Thiamin; its absence causes beriberi.

vitamin C: Ascorbic acid; its absence causes scurvy.

warm-blooded animal: An animal that can control its internal temperature and is thereby relatively independent of its outside environment.

white cell: One of several types of cells in blood that act as part of the immune system.

X rays: A form of radiation that can be used to make images of the inside of the body; in large doses, they can cause serious damage.

yang: An element in traditional Chinese medicine said to be masculine, light, active, dry, and hot.

yellow fever: A serious disease caused by a virus and transmitted by mosquitoes.

yin: In traditional Chinese medicine, an element that is the opposite of yang: feminine, dark, passive, moist, and cold.

For Further Reading

Ruth DeJauregui, *100 Medical Milestones That Shaped World History*. San Mateo, CA: Bluewood Books, 1998. Brief descriptions of advances in medicine that affected the course of history; easy reading.

James Cross Giblin, *When Plague Strikes: The Black Death, Smallpox, AIDS*. New York: Harper, 1997. This young adult book discusses these three great epidemic diseases from a social as well as medical standpoint, describing positive and negative ways in which different cultures have reacted to epidemics.

Harry Henderson and Lisa Yount, *The Scientific Revolution*. San Diego: Lucent Books, 1996. Describes scientific advances in the West in the sixteenth through nineteenth centuries; chapter on medicine describes discoveries of blood circulation, bacteria, the role of microorganisms in causing disease, and vaccination to protect against disease; for young adults.

———, *Twentieth Century Science*. San Diego: Lucent Books, 1997. Chapters on medicine cover genetics, antibiotics and other drugs, and surgical advances such as transplants and artificial organs.

Gael Jennings, *Bloody Moments: And Further Highlights from the Astounding History of Medicine*. Willowdale, Ontario, Canada: Firefly Books, 2000. Offbeat history emphasizing the "gross and disgusting" side of medicine; easy reading.

Roberto Margotta, *The History of Medicine*. New York: Smithmark, 1996. Well-illustrated overview of medical history through the early twentieth century; somewhat difficult reading.

Robert Marion, *Learning to Play God: The Coming of Age of a Young Doctor*. New York: Fawcett, 1993. Autobiographical book that describes the education of a modern medical student.

Lisa Yount, *Epidemics*. San Diego: Lucent Books, 2000. Briefly describes the history of epidemic diseases and medicine's attempts to overcome them but focuses mostly on diseases that threaten the world today; young adult.

———, *Medical Technology*. New York: Facts On File, 1998. Biographical sketches of seven scientists who invented medical technology in the nineteenth and twentieth centuries, including William Morton (anesthesia), Wilhelm Röntgen (X rays), and Karl Landsteiner (blood transfusions).

Works Consulted

Books

Melvin Berger, *The Artificial Heart*. New York: Franklin Watts, 1987. Describes the development of the artificial hearts used in the 1980s and how they work.

Catherine Caufield, *Multiple Exposures*. London: Secker and Warburg, 1989. Describes the discovery, medical uses, and dangers of X rays.

Logan Clendening, ed., *Source Book of Medical History*. Mineola, NY: Dover, 1960. Provides numerous excerpts of primary sources on medical history.

Rob DeSalle, ed., *Epidemic! The World of Infectious Disease*. New York: New Press/American Museum of Natural History, 1999. Well-illustrated, lively text written to accompany a 1999 exhibit by the American Museum of Natural History that described the investigation of epidemic disease; covers both historical and current epidemics.

René Dubos, *The Unseen World*. New York: Rockefeller Institute Press/Oxford University Press, 1962. Describes microorganisms and how Leeuwenhoek, Pasteur, and other scientists learned about them.

Laurence Farmer, *Master Surgeon*. New York: Harper & Brothers, 1962. Short, readable biography of Joseph Lister, the creator of antisepsis.

Meyer Friedman and Gerald W. Friedland, *Medicine's 10 Greatest Discoveries*. New Haven, CT: Yale University Press, 1998. Includes chapters on Vesalius, William Harvey, Antoni Leeuwenhoek, Edward Jenner, Wilhelm Röntgen, and Alexander Fleming.

René Fülöp-Miller, *Triumph over Pain*. Trans. Eden and Cedar Paul. Indianapolis: Bobbs-Merrill, 1938. Dramatic story of the discovery and early development of anesthesia, somewhat fictionalized.

June Goodfield, *Quest for the Killers*. Boston: Birkhäuser, 1985. Includes a chapter on the eradication of smallpox in the 1970s.

William Harvey, *An Anatomical Essay on the Motion of the Heart and Blood in Animals*. Trans. Robert Willis, rev. Alexander Bowie. In the Harvard Classics, *Scientific Papers*, vol. 38. New York: Collier, 1910. Harvey's landmark book describing the circulation of the blood.

Peter Hawthorne, *The Transplanted Heart*. Chicago: Rand McNally, 1968. Describes the dramatic days of the first heart transplants.

Frederic Lawrence Holmes, *Lavoisier and the Chemistry of Life*. Madison: University of Wisconsin Press, 1985. Describes Lavoisier's experiments on respiration and other biological aspects of chemistry.

Samuel Hoole, trans., *The Select Works of Antony van Leeuwenhoek*, vol. 1. New York: Arno Press, 1977. Includes Leeuwenhoek's letters describing microorganisms that he saw under his single-lens microscopes.

Albert S. Lyons and R. Joseph Petrucelli, *Medicine: An Illustrated History*. New York: Abrams, 1987. Extremely well-illustrated history of medicine from earliest times to the early twentieth century.

Andrew Nikiforuk, *The Fourth Horseman: A Short History of Epidemics, Plagues, and Other Scourges*. London: Phoenix, 1993. Describes the past history and present activity of epidemic diseases such as the plague, malaria, smallpox, influenza, and tuberculosis.

W. Robert Nitske, *The Life of Wilhelm Conrad Röntgen*. Tucson: University of Arizona Press, 1971. Biography of the discoverer of X rays.

Roy Porter, *The Greatest Benefit to Mankind: A Medical History of Humanity*. New York: Norton, 1997. Extremely detailed, interesting history of (primarily) Western medicine and its effects on society, including failures as well as triumphs.

Roy Porter, ed., *The Cambridge Illustrated History of Medicine*. Cambridge, England: Cambridge University Press, 1996. Well-illustrated history of medicine, arranged by theme rather than chronology.

Donald Robinson, *The Miracle Finders*. New York: David McKay, 1976. Vividly describes the stories behind twentieth-century medical advances such as the development of antibiotics.

Victoria Sherrow, *Great Scientists*. New York: Facts On File, 1992. For young adults; includes a chapter on James Watson.

Edward Shorter, *The Health Century*. New York: Doubleday, 1987. Interesting account of advances in twentieth-century American medicine, focusing on the government-sponsored National Institutes of Health.

Jane S. Smith, *Patenting the Sun*. New York: William Morrow, 1990. Detailed description of the development of the Salk polio vaccine.

Jenny Sutcliffe and Nancy Duin, *A History of Medicine*. New York: Barnes & Noble, 1992. Well-illustrated history of medicine from earliest times to the 1980s, focusing on the twentieth century.

Larry Thompson, *Correcting the Code*. New York: Simon & Schuster, 1994. Focuses on the first successful gene therapy in 1990 but also describes the advances in molecular biology and genetic engineering that have made gene therapy possible.

René Vallery-Radot, *The Life of Louis Pasteur*. Trans. Mrs. R. L. Devonshire. Garden City, NY: Garden City Publishing, 1927. Detailed, admiring biography of Pasteur by his son-in-law.

James D. Watson, *The Double Helix*. New York: New American Library, 1968.

Lively but biased account of the discovery of the structure of DNA by one of the discoverers.

Allen B. Weisse, *Medical Odysseys: The Different and Sometimes Unexpected Pathways to Twentieth-Century Medical Discoveries.* New Brunswick, NJ: Rutgers University Press, 1991. Includes chapters on antibiotics, the polio vaccine, and heart surgery.

Lael Wertenbaker, *To Mend the Heart: The Dramatic Story of Cardiac Surgery and Its Pioneers.* New York: Viking, 1980. Describes such advances as the heart-lung machine, pacemakers, bypasses, and early heart transplants.

Charles-Edward Amory Winslow, *The Conquest of Epidemic Disease: A Chapter in the History of Ideas.* Madison: University of Wisconsin Press, 1980. Provides many quotes from primary sources to show how thinking about the cause of infectious diseases changed from ancient times to the end of the nineteenth century.

Periodicals

W. French Anderson, "Gene Therapy," *Scientific American*, September 1995.

Associated Press, "AIDS Called Economic Threat in Third World," *San Francisco Chronicle*, November 28, 1997.

John Donnelly, "Chasing Polio to Edges of Earth," *San Francisco Chronicle*, December 24, 2000.

"The Heart: Miracle in Cape Town," *Newsweek*, December 18, 1967.

New York Times, "5.3 Million Got HIV in 2000, Health Group Estimates," *San Francisco Chronicle*, November 25, 2000.

Elizabeth Pennisi, "U.S. Beefs Up CDC's Capabilities," *Science*, June 7, 1996.

Ellen Ruppel Shell, "Return of a Deadly Disease," *Atlantic*, August 1997.

Douglas Starr, "Again and Again in World War II, Blood Made the Difference," *Smithsonian*, March 1995.

Internet Sources

Ralph R. Frerichs, John Snow website, UCLA, Dept. of Epidemiology, School of Public Health, www.ph.ucla.edu/epi/snow.html.

Index

Cope, Richard, 103
Copernicus, Nicolaus, 38
Correcting the Code
   (Thompson), 107
cowpox, 49, 59
Crick, James, 102–103
Crookes tube, 72
culture, 58
cures, 81–83
Curie, Marie and Pierre, 74
cyclosporine, 101
cytoplasm, 63

Davy, Humphry, 68–69
DDT, 95
Descartes, René, 38
deSilva, Ashanthi, 105–106,
   107
diet, 78–80
digestion, 61, 62
digitalis, 46
Dioscorides, 23
diphtheria, 60
dissection
   artists' experience with, 34
   church's views on, 33, 35
   of corpses, 45
   cultural beliefs about, 21
   first regular use of, 21
   by Galen, 23, 24, 36
   at medical schools, 29
   to study circulatory
      system, 39
Dix, Dorothea, 81
DNA, 102–104, 105
Domagk, Gerhard, 85
double helix, 102
dreams, 82
dropsy, 46
drugs
   during early surgeries, 68
   introduced by Paracelsus,
      33
   introduced during
      Enlightenment, 46
   Muslims' knowledge
      about, 28
   sulfa, 85
   see also specific drugs
Dumas, J. B. H., 78

Ebola fever, 99
Edwin Smith papyrus, 15
Egypt, 14–15
Ehrlich, Paul, 84–85
Eijkmann, Christiaan, 78–79
electricity, 44
elephantiasis, 75
encyclopedias
   Ayurvedic, 15–16
   Hebrew and Arabic, 27
   Latin, 28
   written by Celsus, 22–23
Engels, Friedrich, 50
Enlightenment, 43–49
epidemics
   AIDS, 96–99
   Black Death, 29–32
   bubonic plague, 29, 37
   Chadwick's research on,
      52–53
   early theories about,
      31–32
   HIV, 97–99
   during industrial
      revolution, 50
   malaria, 75–76, 77, 95–96
   pneumonic plague, 31
   polio, 88–90, 91
   in sixteenth century, 37
   theories about, 51–52
   treating and preventing,
      50–60
   from tropical diseases,
      75–78
   yellow fever, 75–78
   see also cholera
Erichsen, John, 71
ether, 69, 70
*Experiments and Observations
   on the Gastric Juice*
   (Beaumont), 61, 62

Fabiola, 25
Finlay, Carlos, 76
Fleming, Alexander, 86
Florey, Howard, 87, 88
fractures, 56
free association, 81
Freud, Sigmund, 81–83
Funk, Casimir, 79–80

Galen
   background of, 23–24
   beliefs of
      about blood, 38–39
      about infections, 55
      in observation, 23
   dissections by, 23, 24, 36
   longstanding authority of,
      24, 47
   study of
      in medical schools, 29
      during Renaissance, 32
   translations of works by,
      27
   used drugs for healing, 23
Galilei, Galileo, 38
Gallo, Robert, 97
Galvani, Luigi, 44
gene therapy, 101–106, 107
genetic engineering, 104–106
genetics, 102
genome, 101
Georg Evers papyrus, 14–15
germs. *See* microorganisms
germ theory of disease, 58,
   63–64
Gibbor, John, 93–94
Golden Square, 53
Grassi, Giovanni, 76
*Greatest Benefit to Mankind: A
   Medical History of
   Humanity* (Porter), 19, 41,
   52, 56
Greenlees, James, 56
guilds, 29
Gutenberg, Johannes, 32
Guthrie, Charles, 99

Haller, Albrecht von, 44
Halsted, William, 71
Hammurabi, 14
   Code of, 15, 17
harmony, 16–18
Harvey, William, 38–40, 41
healers
   in ancient times, 13–14
   distrust of, 48
   gods as, 13, 18–19
   history of, 10
   knowledge gained from,
      33

lack of respect for, 10, 29
priests as, 14
reliance on, 47–48
Health Century (Shorter), 89
heartbeat (pulse), 18
heart disease, 99
heart-lung machine, 93–94
heart surgery, 93–94
heart transplants, 100–101, 103
Heatley, Norman, 87
Helmholtz, Hermann von, 67
Helmont, Jan Baptista van, 44
Henle, Jacob, 59
Herodotus, 15
Hinduism, 15
Hippocrates, 19–22
Hippocratic oath, 21, 22
History of Medicine (Margotta), 34
HIV (human immunodeficiency virus), 97–99
Holmes, Oliver Wendell, 70
homeostasis, 64
Hooke, Robert, 62–63
hospitals
established by Muslims, 28
first, in history, 25
government control over, 29
medical training in, 47
for mentally ill, 81, 82
human testing, 94
humors, 20–21, 23, 47

illness
chronic, 99
early beliefs about
caused by
body and environment, 19–20
disturbed harmony, 16–18
gods and supernatural beings, 13, 18–19, 25

inbalance of humors, 20–21
Imhotep, 15, 18
immune system, 99–100
see also AIDS; HIV
immunologists, 100
industrial revolution, 50
infections, 55–58
infectious diseases
in twenty-first century, 95–99
see also epidemics; *specific diseases*
influenza, 88
Inner Canon of Medicine (Yu Hsing), 16–17
Islam, 27

Janssen, Hans and Zacharias, 40
Jenner, Edward, 49, 59
Jesuits' bark, 46
Jung, Carl, 83

Kitasato, Shibasaburo, 60
Koch, Robert, 59–60
Koller, Carl, 71
Kraepelin, Emil, 81

Laënnec, René, 66, 67
Lancet (medical journal), 56
Landsteiner, Karl, 91–92
Laveran, Charles, 75
Lavoisier, Antoine, 44–45
Leeuwenhoek, Antoni van, 42–43, 58
Leonardo da Vinci, 33, 34, 35
Liebig, Justus von, 61
life expectancy, 12, 60
Life of Wilhelm Conrad Röntgen (Nitske), 74
lifestyle
advocates of healthy
Chinese physicians, 17
Hippocrates, 21
modern doctors, 107
Salerno medical school, 30
Lind, James, 79–80
Lister, Joseph, 54–58

Long, Crawford, 70

Maimonides, 27
malaria
causes of, 75–76, 77
epidemics of, 75–76, 77, 95–96
malnutrition, 78–80
Malpighi, Marcello, 40–42
Manson, Patrick, 75
Marx, Karl, 50
McClure's Magazine, 73
medical schools
dissections at, 29
first, in history, 29
growth in numbers of, 29
in Salerno, 29, 30
medical training
in anatomy, 36
in hospitals, 47
role of observation in, 23, 24, 46–47
medicine
Ayurvedic, 15–16
Chinese
beliefs and treatments in, 15–18
medical theories of, 20–21
human testing and, 94
importance of anatomy to, 36
Indian
beliefs and treatments in 15–18
medical theories behind, 20–21
nineteenth-century advances in, 10–11
religious groups' control over, 25–29
role of, 10
symbol of, 18
tropical, 75
twentieth-century advances in, 11–12
Western, 19, 21
Medicine: An Illustrated History (Lyons and Petrucelli), 17

Picture Credits

About the Author

Lisa Yount earned a bachelor's degree with honors in English and creative writing from Stanford University. She has a lifelong interest in biology and medicine. She has been a professional writer and editor for almost thirty-five years, producing educational materials, magazine articles, and thirty books for young adults and adults. Her books for Lucent include *Disease Detectives*, *Epidemics*, and *Cancer*. She lives in El Cerrito, California, with her husband, a large library, and several cats.